BE
YOUR
OWN
DICK

Private Investigating
Made Easy

John Q. Newman

Loompanics Unlimited
Port Townsend, Washington

John Q. Newman is the author of these other fine books available from Loompanics Unlimited:

- **The Heavy Duty New Identity**
- **Understanding U.S. Identity Documents**

This book is sold for information purposes only. Neither the author nor the publisher will be held accountable for the use or misuse of the information contained in this book.

Published by:

Loompanics Unlimited
P.O. Box 1197
Port Townsend, WA 98368

Loompanics Unlimited is a division of Loompanics Enterprises, Inc.

ISBN 1-55950-083-2
Library of Congress Catalog Card Number 92-070018

Table
of
Contents

Introduction

This book is designed to allow almost any person to do investigative work on individuals from the comfort of their home. In many ways this book is the alter-ego of other books on establishing a new identity or increasing your personal privacy. Establishing a new identity essentially involves re-plugging oneself into all of the various databases that validate one's existence. The new personal particulars isolate the "new" you from your old self.

These same databases can be tapped by the person who wishes to do the opposite, that is, to invade the privacy of others. In the age of computerized files and databases, this can be done very easily. The moral implications of such actions are left to the individual. But before the reader makes a hasty value judgment, consider this.

Have you ever wondered how a rival long distance telephone company "knew" you spent $25 a month on long distance calls to Japan? Have you ever wondered how a credit card company "knew" you would be a good prospect for their credit card, or how an insurance company "knew" you were in need of new auto insurance? To one extent or another these corporations invaded your personal privacy by consulting certain databases and other information sources that contained personal details on you. Having done this, they then determined you were a likely candidate for their product and service. Most people simply do not know that this is what is being done.

Other books have been written on this subject, but all too often they have detailed methods and systems that are either too arcane and expensive to be used by the average person, or they detail procedures that will almost certainly lead the reader into a confrontation with the law. This book will explain what 90% of private detective work involves doing. That is, collecting data on a "target" or person.

$$\boxed{1}$$

TV
vs.
Reality

When a person mentions "investigations" or "private detective," certain images immediately come to mind. Popular television shows such as *Simon and Simon*, *Magnum P.I.* and others picture a glorious and adventure-filled life for the private detective investigator. A typical case scenario tends to unfold along the following line of action.

Late one night our hero, the investigator, gets a telephone call that a sister of a friend of a friend has vanished. The police have not got a clue as to why the woman has suddenly disappeared. The next morning our hero is fast on the case. A first-class plane ride to the missing woman's former home is sure to follow with a chat with the woman's relative. While here, our hero has rented a very fast and expensive sports car. This is in case he will need to do some fast getaway driving when he starts making inquiries of the wrong people.

Soon thereafter our hero will return to his home base. His own personal transportation will likely be a $30,000-plus sports car. No doubt our hero will have an underworld contact, another "friend of a friend," who can give him another piece to the puzzle. Acting on this new knowledge, our hero contacts the wrong person, and some very nasty gunplay develops. Of course, our hero is unhurt, and when the police arrive on the scene, he is merely questioned and later released.

When the case is finally over, it will turn out that the missing woman was involved with a real rogue bunch. It comes out that she was the girlfriend of a big-time drug importer and that she found out too much for her own good. A disagreement between rival drug import-ers erupted, and she was sacrificed in the crossfire. Our hero helps bring the guilty parties to justice. Later on, the woman's saddened but grateful parents reward our hero with a huge fee.

What an exciting and action-packed life the investi-gator leads! First class air travel, fancy cars, good looking women, (Oh, I forgot to mention that our hero has a 36-24-36 girlfriend who puts up with his crap, but is always there for his convenience.), not to mention gunplay and fat paychecks. Well, welcome to reality. This kind of fantasy may make for good tele-vision, but the real world of the investigator is much different than the fantasy world portrayed on tele-vision. Investigator or private detective work is all about the same basic commodity: accurate informa-tion about people.

The investigator's job is to uncover information about the location or condition or activities of persons of interest. The type of investigators portrayed on television bear no relation at all to reality. Even the few agencies that perform this type of dangerous work will be the first to tell you that when gunplay or fights start, it usually means that an investigator is doing his job improperly. The first rule of an investigator is stealth and discretion. The very fact that an investigation is going on and data being collected is something that should not be known to the subject.

The type of investigations we will be looking at focus on at-a-distance methods that can be employed by you at your present location. Investigators can do various types of work. Unclaimed property, for example, is a very good one. Each year thousands of people are located by investigators who can give them the happy news that they are owners of unclaimed property. Naturally, the investigator collects a percentage. Bank loan departments and automobile finance companies are other good examples of places where a free-lance investigator can find profitable work. Once these institutions know where a deadbeat is, they can repossess their collateral.

Utility companies, the telephone company, etc., need reliable investigators who can give good results. Frequently when people move they forget to claim their deposits back from these services. This creates a headache for the company involved because they are legally liable to keep account of this money and the interest it accrues until it is paid out to the owner.

What should be clear is that most of an investigator's working time is spent behind a desk, in front of a book, or computer. Investigation is about information, not fast cars, sexy women and guns!

$$\boxed{2}$$

Information
is
Everywhere

People leave an ever growing paper trail in life. The only person who cannot be found is a person who has made a deliberate decision to change his identity and follows through with the necessary details. But in some cases, you may wish, not to find someone, but to uncover personal information about someone you already know. This could be for any number of reasons. It turns out that it is becoming increasingly popular for unmarried women to hire private detectives to do background investigations of potential husbands. Your reasons are your own private matter. My objective is to show you how to properly organize and execute a search.

Let's go back to what I said about leaving a "paper trail" in life. Consider for a moment all of the personal data that *you* have freely provided to complete strangers. If you have a drivers license, the State Motor Vehicle department has your name and number. The credit bureau has you on file if you have ever applied for credit, regardless of whether it was actually received. Do you vote, have medical insurance, or work in a licensed profession? If so, there are places which contain surprisingly detailed information about you. If you have a dog that has a license, a person could learn much about you from this source.

Before you scoff or laugh at my suggestions, a couple of real-life examples are in order. A few years back the FBI decided that foreign nationals were posing a grave threat to the national security of the United States. How were these dangerous agents doing this? By using the public library. In 1985 the FBI started its innocent sounding "Library Awareness Program." This program involved the FBI visiting about 100 major U.S. public and university libraries. The FBI requested that the head librarian in each institution forward to the FBI the name, birthdate, address, and book check-out file of any borrower who "appeared" to be "foreign" and whose reading list contained books that might be "sensitive."

What did the FBI consider to be sensitive? Any library books regarding nuclear power, aerospace, high technology in general, and a slew of other subjects under the heading of "inappropriate in the librarian's eyes." To the librarians' credit, the FBI was rebuffed at *almost* every turn. Finally the "Library Awareness Program" was dropped because of the negative stories in the media.

However, many innocent Americans now have files established on them at FBI headquarters because they have "foreign sounding" names and read "sensitive" books. The few librarians that did agree to supply the information requested were cowed by the FBI agents hinting that if they did not cooperate, the *librarians* themselves would become the subject of negative data files at the FBI. The files established on these citizens would then be "fleshed out" with information from other databases.

Consider what can be learned about an individual from his library card files. There is the data collected from you when you established your borrower status. This would contain, at the least, your name, birthdate, telephone number, address, and the number and type of identity document used to prove your residence. Your book borrowing file would contain the dates of your visits to the library, what type of reading material you check out, late fines, and how often you go to the library.

This data itself, although it reveals little about you, is not all that private. But consider how this data can be electronically cross linked to other databases, which brings us to our next true-life example.

In 1987 there was heated debate about a U.S. Supreme Court nominee. Ironically enough, this judge who was nominated to the U.S. Supreme Court did not believe that the United States Constitution created any type of privacy rights. The nomination failed in large part due to the controversy over the privacy rights issue. The nominee was a great fan of video rental stores and in the melee around the nomination someone managed to get a hold of the nominee's movie rental records. His movie rental records were harmless, but much controversy ensued over how these records were obtained. In reaction to this, the United States Congress passed a law that now protects an individual's video store rental records more completely than almost any other privately collected database in the nation. The credit bureau can release your credit report to just about anyone, but the proprietor of a video store can face jail and a fine if he releases video rental records without a court order.

The purpose of these two examples is to illustrate just how much information is available on people at seemingly innocuous places. You can learn how to efficiently and effectively tap into these information sources.

Let's assume one night you are watching your local evening newscast and a major event has taken place and reporters are doing "on the street" opinion interviews. From the quick chat you are able to obtain a subject's name and city of residence. Our objective will be to put together a complete dossier on his life for the last 2 years or so. Let's call him Bill Jones and we will say he is from Portland, Oregon. How can we learn all about Bill?

The investigation techniques in this book work because most people do certain things in life. A person's paper trail in life begins with a birth certificate and ends with a death certificate. In between there are reams of paperwork one must compile to function. Even if a given individual has managed to avoid one or two databases, another one will surely contain nuggets of data. The key is to accumulate data bit by bit until you have the big picture. The first step is to compile a worksheet like the one illustrated in Appendix 1.

The worksheet allows you to fill in what is known about the target and then to systematically work from there. We know our subject is a resident of the Portland, Oregon area and that his first and last names are Bill Jones. You should also jot down the personal appearance details that you remember. His hair color, eye color, weight and approximate height are all important. Also notice if he has a detectable accent of any kind. The key to investigation of any kind is close attention to details.

The next chapter will give you an overview of potential sources of data and how to use them. After you are acquainted with these data sources, we will then investigate "Bill Jones" by going through each information source systematically.

3

Data Sources
and
Methods

This chapter is designed to show you how to do one thing. That is to collect data on individuals in a timely and organized fashion. This data can be of many types. It can be financial, medical, employment history, or personal data such as marital status and lifestyle. The methods here will locate and provide information on 99.5% of people.

These methods are based on the following principle: *Almost all people must interact with certain agencies to function.* We are usually able to find the person of interest, or to learn more about their personal habits and background. Most people wrongly assume that their files with these agencies are private, when in reality they are open for inspection to all who request them. A good example and excellent starting point is to examine the Motor Vehicle Departments of most states and see what we can learn about a person from them.

Most people will interact with their state's Motor Vehicle Department. This is for two reasons. The first is that most Americans will learn how to drive a car, and that means a drivers license. The second is that the Motor Vehicle Department administers the issuance of state identity cards in most states. Because people generally want to have one piece of state-issued identification, people who do not drive often get a state identity card instead. The Motor Vehicle Department is a "soft touch" when it comes to data exchange. But first, let's see just what they know about an individual.

A person's Motor Vehicle Department file has two parts to it. The first part is the base identification file. This part of the file consists of the basic personal information provided upon an individual's first contact with the Motor Vehicle Department. This part of the file will also usually contain information on the supportive documentation that was presented as proof of identity.

The second part of the Motor Vehicle Department file consists of the individual's driving record. This is the "active" part of the file that is updated whenever an input is made into the system. For example, the file will be updated to show that a person received a speeding ticket or was involved in an accident. The driver record will include the current address of the driver, the total of all moving violations, current insurance information, current license information, change of name data, and any driving while drunk or vehicular homicide convictions as well. Some states will include an actual photocopy of the drivers license and the application form when the driving record is obtained.

Most people falsely believe that a person's driving record is only available to other states' Motor Vehicle Departments, automobile insurance companies, and law enforcement personnel. Nothing could be more inaccurate than this. Practically every state will sell to anyone a copy of a person's driving record. In fact, most states sell all changes of address stored in the

Motor Vehicle Department computers to national firms that advertise they can update addresses nation-wide. You might wonder how this state of affairs came to pass.

In short, the motive was greed and profits. The automobile insurance industry is the reason that there is no privacy in Motor Vehicle Department records anymore. The next time you receive one of those "pre-approved" offers for low cost automobile insurance, you can thank the Motor Vehicle Department for pro-viding the data. The automobile insurance industry creates profits by identifying the bad drivers and no longer insuring them, and by searching out the good driver and writing him a policy. Searching motor vehicle records allows this.

What happens is the insurance companies will run large scale checks of all drivers in a particular state's database. This can be further narrowed by singling out certain groups of drivers. For example, the insurance company could ask for a listing of drivers over 35 years old with no accidents for the last 5 years. This tailored computer search would then provide all the names of drivers meeting these criteria. Clearly, for an investi-gator, the Motor Vehicle Department is a very useful source of data. But how do you access it?

Appendix 2 contains the addresses of the central Motor Vehicle Department offices for all fifty states. It is from these offices that requests for driving records are handled. Most states have a preprinted form you use to run a search-all. You must submit this form, along with the current fee, and you will have an answer back in a few days, allowing for the mailing time. Your first order of business should be to send a letter to these addresses asking for a request form and the current fee. The request form you can photocopy, and you should set up an alphabetical file for these. You should understand the different types of searches that can be provided for you.

The most useful search is called an "alpha" search, "alpha" being short for alphabetical. An alpha search simply means you have a name and you want the database to be checked to see if anyone by that name, and possibly address or birth date, has a license from this state. The other type of search is called a numeric search. On a numeric search, you may have a license number and you want to find out the driver's name and driving record that goes with it.

The other side of the driving record is vehicle registration information. In the United States we have a two level system in operation on vehicle registration data. In most states, when a person goes to register a car, one does not go to the Motor Vehicle Department, but to the local county registrar or auditor's office. License plates and registration documents are assigned from here. But the Motor Vehicle branch central computer maintains a data file on all vehicles registered in the state. This is the database that a police officer consults when he pulls over a vehicle. The vehicle registration index will contain the details of the vehicle serial number and body style, along with the registered owner's name and address and the legal owner's name and address.

In the United States, most states issue a title document to a car. The original of this document will be on file at the county courthouse or county auditor's office in the county of vehicle registration. These are public documents. The vehicle title shows who the owner in the legal sense is, and if there are any liens on the vehicle.

We now will examine four directories which you will find very useful. They are the telephone directory, the City Directory, the Criss-Cross Directory and the phone locator directory. When one knows how to efficiently use these directories, information about a person can generally be readily found. The telephone directory is the most obvious. It is surprising how many people can be located very quickly through the telephone directory. Usually people make the mistake of not being careful enough when they use it. For example, in many larger cities, the city and the surrounding area have two separate sets of white pages. Another fact to keep in mind is that in many areas an unlisted number just means it is not available from directory assistance. The same number may still be in the telephone book unless a person purchases the unlisted and non-published option.

The next directory to look at is the Criss-Cross Directory. This directory is one the telephone company does not publicize. A Criss-Cross Directory lists all telephone numbers in a given street or section of a city. A Criss-Cross will even list non-published numbers. If you have an idea a person lives within a certain block, you could go to the telephone Criss-Cross Directory and get the number of every telephone on this block. You then use another little-known directory to see if that person does live there. This directory is called the telephone locator, and it is the alter-ego of the Criss-Cross directory.

The telephone locator lists all telephones by sequential number, arranged by the exchange number. For example, in the 872 exchange, it would start out with 872-0000, then 0001, etc. Beside each listing will be the address of the number, and to whom the telephone is listed.

These directories are all very useful. What is nice for an investigator is that he need not purchase them outright. Often, the local library branch has them on the shelf and you can use them there.

The single best directory, which you will find yourself consulting all the time, is known as the City Directory. The City Directory has nothing to do with the telephone company. This directory provides a wealth of information about individuals that can be linked to other databases.

The City Directory collects its data from landlords, telephone books, employees and, not surprisingly, the people concerned themselves. One way they achieve such a high degree of compliance is the confusion between themselves and the telephone directory. City Directory canvassers are told to feed on this sense of confusion. If a canvasser cannot get the required information from the person concerned, then, for example, in the case of apartment dwellers, they will contact the landlord. City Directories contain a large amount of data on the individuals listed.

A City Directory listing will contain an individual's full address. The listing also tells the nature of the accommodation. For example, codes on the listing will indicate if a person rents an apartment, whether it is furnished or unfurnished, or in the case of a house, if the person owns it or is merely boarding. As one can see, a City Directory listing can provide a quick way to find out other useful information about people.

City Directories are published for almost every city and town in the United States. For larger metropolitan areas there are two directories. There will be one directory for the central city and another one for the suburban regions. You cannot purchase the directory outright. You must lease it, or use one available at a library. City Directories are a key tool in getting information quickly and cheaply on people who have non-listed, non-published telephone numbers, or have only "occupant" listed on their apartment building directories. The other utility of City Directory listings is to allow you to trace a person's history relatively easily in a given area.

For example, let's say you are doing a background check on "Bill Jones." You go to this year's City Directory and obtain his current address. You would then go to past editions of the City Directory, conveniently located at the local library, and look under his name. Each year's listing will contain his address at the time, his employer at the time, and other useful data. At some point his listing will disappear. When this occurs, check the suburban editions. Unless he left the area, his name will likely be in the suburban directory.

Another reason for the usefulness of the City Directory is in its ability to allow you to gather data on people who are related to your target individual. A City Directory listing will tell you if a person is married, and if so, the name of the spouse. If, when you are doing your search, the listing for the husband disappears, check for a separate listing for the wife. The same can be done on children of the subject, co-workers, etc. Using the City Directory wisely allows you to find many people quickly and at a minimum of expense.

Another easily consulted source of information is the voter registration list. Voter registration lists are public records in every state. A voter registration listing will usually contain the person's full name, date of birth, address, and sometimes telephone number and employer. A copy of the local voters list can usually be found at a local branch library, and always at the county clerk's office.

The Social Security number is also a very useful piece of information to have. Even in states where a drivers license does not share the Social Security number, it is often requested and recorded into the DMV computer. A numeric search can often be run by just knowing the Social Security number. The same is true of auto registration listings. Many states require a person wishing to register a car to provide the Social Security number. A check of the vehicle registration database can often be run this way. Secondly, Social Security numbers can provide a way to learn about a person's background. The first 3 digits of a Social Security number are called an area number. Every state is assigned a different set of these area numbers. Appendix 3 shows the number series in use for the various states. Thus, a Social Security number can direct your search to a different state.

Another way that Social Security numbers can be useful is if you can identify a death claim number. The Social Security Administration has started to compile a history of all "retired" Social Security numbers, "retired" being a nice way of saying "dead." Retired Social Security numbers are purchased from the government by a couple of private companies that then resell these numbers.

The largest private databases in the nation are run by the four large nationwide credit bureaus. Very often good information can be obtained on a person, when other methods have failed, by tapping into this network. Until recently, these databanks were off limits to an investigator. However, recent Federal Government decisions now make some of this information available to the investigator. Let's see what the particulars are.

Credit bureau reports contain three types of information on them. The first is called "header" information. Header information is the personal data that appears at the top of the credit report. This is what allows the computer to find a certain file. Header data includes full name, address, date of birth, telephone number, and on some reports, employer. The second section of a credit bureau report contains the credit history itself. Here you will find a listing of all charge and credit accounts, along with their payment history and balance. The bottom portion of the credit report contains the recording of any tax liens, bankruptcy or other financially motivated legal action.

Recent decisions allow credit bureaus to sell off header information on individuals for any purpose. Previously, this data could only be released for the purpose of granting credit or for employment where a person's financial standing was an important consideration. To understand the utility of credit header information, one must understand how the National Credit Reporting system works.

Whenever an individual applies for credit, a two step process begins. The first step is called credit scoring. When an application is scored, a number of factors, such as income, type of employment, etc., are examined. Every creditor has their own definition as to what makes a good risk. If an application passes through this initial screening, a credit bureau report is obtained. The credit bureau report acts as the final check. A credit bureau report allows the creditor to avoid going through the time and expense of calling each reference on the application to verify the details.

The largest credit bureau network in the United States is run by TRW of Cleveland, Ohio. They have credit files on almost 130 million people, and offices all across the United States. Two other large credit bureaus are Credit Bureau Incorporated, CBI for short, and the Transunion Credit Bureau. Almost all local credit bureaus are either owned by these companies outright, or they are affiliated with them in some way.

When a creditor checks on an application, he provides the credit bureau computer with the "header" data from the application. The credit bureau's central computer will then attempt to find a match based on an internal identification code. This code uses parts of the person's name, birthdate, address, marital status and social security number to attempt a match. If no match is found, a new credit file with the "header" data from the application is created. If a file already exists, it is matched up to the new application, and the address portion of the header information is updated.

This is the reason for the great utility of credit bureau header data in performing address searches on people. Credit reports are often run by landlords and employers, without the subject being aware of it. If someone you are looking for has moved and attempts to rent an apartment, there is a good chance a credit report will be obtained. By plugging into the credit bureau computer, you will be in a position to obtain this data. To do this you will need to go through a third party service, which will be explained later.

Another good source of data is the county real estate index and local courthouse litigation index. More detail on how these records work is provided in Chapters 7 and 8.

Now we will proceed with our investigation of Bill Jones, and we will show how to use all of the aforementioned databases in a coherent way.

$$\boxed{4}$$

Telephone Books
and
City Directories

We need more basic information about Bill Jones, such as an address and telephone number. Once armed with these we can find out additional data more easily. The first place to look is in the telephone directory. This may seem pretty obvious, but it is amazing how few people think to do this. We know that our target resides somewhere in the Portland area. We would want to check not only the city of Portland telephone book, but also the phone books of neighboring suburban areas. Next you must keep in mind that Bill can be short for William. On your worksheet you will allow a space to list any common variants of the target's name, and check for these. Now what happens if you cannot find a telephone listing? In fact, let's suppose that he has deliberately gotten an unlisted number.

First, you will want to exhaust all possible telephone company leads. This is another important aspect of mounting an effective and timely investigation. *Do not move on to another source until have you milked the current one dry.* A person who has an unlisted number may still be contacted in many cases by calling information directly. This varies a bit from phone company to phone company. Some telephone companies say that with them an unlisted number means that the number is only not published (listed) in the phone book. These phone companies also have a *non-published, and non-listed* option. But we will further assume that you still cannot get a telephone number on Mr. Jones even after calling information. What is your next move?

The first place you will consult is the *City Directory*. As I said in Chapter 3, this directory has nothing to do with the telephone company. Perhaps you have been accosted at home on a Saturday afternoon by a neighborhood woman and asked questions about your name, marital status, place of work and ownership of the property. The canvasser, if you had asked, would only say she worked for the "city directory." Most people upon hearing this drop all defense of their privacy and happily answer all questions, thinking it is for the telephone book. Information for the city directory is also obtained from landlords, state drivers license files, and from the telephone company itself.

City directories are published by private corporations. The two largest publishers are R.L. Polk and Coles Householder. The directories are organized into two sections. One section will be indexed according to street location and the other is by alphabetical name. Often a large metropolitan area will have more than one city directory. There will be a city directory for the main city and a suburban directory for the outlying areas as well. A city directory listing that is complete will provide a virtual gold mine of information on a person. A complete listing will show the complete name of the person, his street address, whether it is an apartment or house, and further if it is rented or owned by the person. A code will also list about how long the person has lived there.

The history will also detail the person's marital status, and the name of the spouse and any dependents who may live there. A complete listing will also have the employer's name and the person's job title. Sometimes, however, the listing is not complete, but it will almost always get you started.

We know our subject's name, so that is where we would look first. There are liable to be a lot of Bill or William Joneses. Usually the person you are looking for does not have such a common name. But when this is the case, you refer back to the little you do know about the target to narrow the candidates down. For example, our target may have been interviewed (on TV) after work. Clearly a listing that shows a Bill Jones as retired isn't the man you seek. By the same token, a listing for a Bill Jones who is a student is not your target. Once you have narrowed down your list of candidates by eliminating those who are obviously not your man, consider more subtle points.

Where was he interviewed? If it was in downtown Portland after work or on his lunch hour, a history for a Bill Jones who works at a company 20 miles out in the suburbs is probably not your man. How to check company locations? Look in the phone book or in the city directory again. The point I am driving at is there are many possible strategies to follow, depending upon what data you do know. For example, let's say our man was interviewed at home in the suburbs by our man-in-the-street reporter, but when checking the alphabetical city directory listing, you find nothing.

If you are able to pinpoint the general area that he is in, you have a number of options. The first is to turn to the street listings for his community and search them until you find his name. This is the other listing in the city directory we mentioned earlier. Another approach is to then use the *phone locator*. Once again, exhaust your city directory *first* before moving on to your next information source.

The phone locator is another privately published directory. As I explained in Chapter 3, it lists telephone numbers sequentially, arranged by the exchange. By each number there will be an address and the name of the person there. If you know the general area where your target resides, it is an easy matter to look in the phone book for the exchange or exchanges that serve the area. Once you have this, you would consult the phone locator listings under these exchanges and scan the listings until you have found your man. So armed with a telephone number and address for our Bill Jones, you can proceed to learn more, but before we do, I want to mention another source of basic personal data.

The local voters list is available at the local library, as are the city directory and phone locator directory. The voters list will give you the local address, which will then allow you to obtain the phone number and other personal data from the city directory and phone locator. These are sources for only basic data. These sources will not give you the intimate details of your target's life, but they put you on the fast track to getting it. The other thing is that these information sources are available free of charge at the local library. (If, by some chance, you don't find the local voters list at the library, then try the county clerk's office.)

So we now have our target's name, home address, telephone number. We should also know if our target rents an apartment or rents/owns a house. But our thirst for knowledge has just begun to be slaked. One added point: sometimes you will not find a listing in the current city directory, phone locator or voters list. When this occurs, go to the stacks and use a copy of last year's and previous years' directories. Almost always this will yield good results, and as an added dividend it can tell you about previous addresses and phone numbers.

$$\boxed{5}$$

Motor Vehicles
and
Drivers Licenses

Almost everyone has dealings with the state Motor Vehicle Department. Drivers must obtain their licenses from this agency, and non-drivers often obtain a state identification card from the same source. The other side of the driving license picture is Motor Vehicle Registration. Most people who drive own a car. Car ownership generates at least two documents in most states. The car title is the real property deed of the vehicle. The other document is the vehicle registration which is the license for the car to be driven on public roadways. By tapping into these sources, we can unearth much more about Mr. Jones.

Let's start with vehicle registration and title records. Titles for vehicles are usually filed at the county courthouse where the car was produced or where the owner lives. The vehicle title will show the name of the purchaser, his address, vehicle license number, if any, the serial number of the vehicle, and, if the vehicle was financed, the name of the lender holding liens on the car. The easiest way to proceed is to run a check on the vehicle registration and then use this data to find the title. An added bonus of vehicle registration data is it often will contain the drivers license number of the registered owner. The wonderful aspect of vehicle registration records is anyone can run a registration check.

We know that Mr. Jones lives in Portland, Oregon and we can assume at this point that if he has any cars, they carry Oregon registrations on them. Your check back a year or two in the city directory confirmed this. The type of search you will want to run is called an "alpha" search. This will search by name and address all vehicles registered to this person. Many states require a person to give a Social Security number when they register a vehicle, and often this number is on the registration form. So it is quite likely that you can obtain the subject's Social Security number from the alpha search. Once you have the vehicle registration information you can then obtain a copy of the title from the local county courthouse. Vehicle registration data is almost universally available in all states to anyone. If one particular state gives you some bureaucratic runaround, you can always check out a car from that state by doing it through another state that has more open access to its records.

While we are running the vehicle search at the vehicle license office, we can open a similar search on the driving license front. Driving license data consists of two parts. The first part is the information actually provided to obtain the license on the application. The second part is the driving record. Some states allow anyone access to both types of data on the premise that it is public information. Some states restrict access to driver license application data to law enforcement personnel. Regardless of the policy you can get the data you need. Because state identity cards are often issued by the Motor Vehicle Department, you can have access to this data as well for a non-driver.

Let's look first at states where driver license application data is available to anyone. In Appendix 2 there is a listing of Motor Vehicle Driver License offices by state. You would write or call them requesting information on the current fee for doing a search. Once you have this you would send your request for all driver license/state identity card application information on file. What you will receive is a very detailed look at our Mr. Jones.

The application data will show his name, birthdate, Social Security number, place of birth, mother's and father's names, and most importantly, the documents used to prove his identity. This will almost always include a previous drivers license or state identity card and his birth certificate number and state of issue. Some states even want your marital status.

What happens if you are dealing with a state that wants to restrict this type of data? You have two choices. The first is to go through a private company that is able to obtain this data for a fee. These firms are listed in Appendix 4.

But I recommend you try option two before you pay another party to accomplish what you can do at a lesser price. Even in states where the official policy is "police access only," the reality is totally different. Go spend $20 and have some letterhead and business cards/envelopes printed up with an official sounding title, such as "Personnel Verification Corporation," or something similar. Send a typewritten letter requesting a copy of the driver application data along with the required fee, stating in the letter that it is needed for "background verification purposes." You will receive a reply quickly.

Driving record data is handled differently, primarily because of the auto insurance industry. Auto insurers want people with bad driving records off the highways as soon as possible. The only way to do this is to have free and easy access to a person's driving record. That is why you will get pre-approved auto insurance offers if your driving record is good. The state motor vehicle department has sold your story.

Appendix 5 lists the addresses for each state's accident report files. The driving record will contain details of all moving violations, citations, license suspensions and accidents or drunk driving records. In the case of accidents, the driving record will list the accident report number. For citations, a citation number is listed. Where a criminal charge resulted from an accident, such as drunken driving, a court file will be listed as well. The excellent aspect of this is all of these records are public domain. The driving record is available from the same place as the driver license application form data. First get the driving record data, then write for specific accident reports or citation data.

So what more do we know about Mr. Jones now? Quite a bit. We know where he was born, where he lived before coming to Portland, if he is a good driver, and what kind of car he has. We also know if his car was financed, and if so, by whom. We might also know if he is married or not. We might know that he has a drinking problem if he has several alcohol-related citations. But the picture is far from complete. We must press onward!

6

The
Home Front

It might be useful to find out more about Mr. Jones's home and family life. We should find out something about his parents and if he has any brothers or sisters. If you recall when we obtained a copy of his drivers license application or state identity card application, we were given details of his date and place of birth and the names of his parents. We should then contact the state vital statistics office in his place of birth and request the long-form certificate of birth.

The long-form certificate of birth is very rarely used by people. It is too big and bulky, so most people just purchase a short form when they need a birth certificate. The long-form certificate is much better for our purposes because it will contain details about Bill's parents, and other information. You have enough information to request Bill's birth certificate in his name if you so desire. As with driver license application data, states vary in their policy about third party birth certificate requests. Many states treat birth records as public domain documents, others do not. In reality, there is no need to apply in Bill's name if it makes you uncomfortable. In restrictive states, simply send one of your letterhead letters saying that a copy of the certificate is needed for "U.S. birth verification." Your request will be honored at once. A listing of all state vital records offices is included in Appendix 6. Write first and find out the current fee and availability policy. This saves you time later on.

With the long-form of Bill's birth certificate — and we should now call him Bill because we know him so well — we can start seeing if he has relatives in the Portland area. A quick check of the city directory and telephone book will tell us if the whole family has relocated to Portland. The birth certificate also allows us to make a quick trace of Bill and his family over the years.

If Bill was born in Indiana, let's say, he had to come to Portland at some point in time. Or it is possible that Bill's parents moved to Portland with him at an early age. The way to run this search is to go back ten or fifteen years in the old Portland city directories. If Bill's parents don't live in Portland, do your first check under Bill's name. Eventually you should reach a year where Bill "drops out" of the city directory. If Bill is married, and the marriage occurred during your search period, Bill's wife will drop out of the city directory listing in that year or the previous year. If Bill's parents now live in Portland, check back on their listing as well. Another approach is to send a letter to the library in the city where Bill was born and ask them to send you a photocopy of the city directory listings of his parents for ten years following his birth, or until the listing "drops off." This gives you a chronological history of the family.

We mentioned that if Bill was married during your search period, his wife's joint listing will vanish at some point. You could then look up his wife's city directory listing as well. When people are married, two sets of data are created. The first set of data is the application data to obtain the marriage license itself. The second set consists of the papers that are sent to the county recorder's office once the marriage has taken place. You can obtain these files as well, if you want them. The only sticking point is knowing the date of the marriage so you don't have to search through a year of files. If you want the data, you can get it.

The city directory listing told us what type of accommodation Bill lives in. Perhaps we would like to learn more about it. If it is rented accommodation, a quick call to the apartment manager will give us his monthly rent and length of tenancy. Landlords blab on everyone, especially if their building is owned by a corporation. You may prefer to use the letter approach, but send it to the office of the real estate company. The company will then send this to the on-site manager to complete and mail to you. In cases like these, always include a self-addressed stamped envelope to facilitate a speedy reply to your letter.

If Bill owns his house we might want to know how many square feet it has, when it was purchased, the purchase price, and what lender provided the financing. These records are in the public domain in every state. The city directory can be a big help in narrowing our search. Note the year that Bill obtained his present address. That is likely the year in which he purchased the property.

Real estate transactions are compiled on an annual basis by the county or city concerned. All persons selling property in a given year are in one volume for the year, and likewise all people buying property in a given year are in another volume. These files will be arranged alphabetically by the last name of the person buying or selling the property. These records are open to public view, and now they may be on microfiche or on computer. The property record will contain the seller's name, the buyer's name (Bill), type of deed issued on the property, the date the deed was granted, which specific book the deed is contained in, how much was paid for the property, and the property location. Guess what? You can now go and get a copy of the deed on Bill's house at the same office. They will be happy to help you. For good measure, get it certified!

We now have the deed to Bill's house and the title to his car, but a lot more of the story of Bill Jones remains to be fleshed out.

7

Finances

We would like to know about Bill's financial picture.
We have made some start in that direction. From the
landlord or property office records we have a good
idea of how much he spends each month to keep a roof
over his head. When we checked out his cars, we found
out he is paying a monthly car payment. It might be
nice to learn his monthly income.

The city directory will have listed his employer and
job title. There are various avenues to get a good
estimate on Bill's income. By having gone back a few
years in the city directory we have a good idea of how
long Bill has been with his present employer. If Bill
works at a unionized company in a job that requires a
union card, we have our answer.

A quick call to the company's personnel office will
tell us which union represents workers who do Bill's
job. After that, telephone the union's local and ask
what the hourly rate was on the last contract settle-
ment at this company. Sometimes you can even get a
copy of the collective agreement. If Bill works in a
salaried professional level job you have a number of
options.

If Bill works in a profession that requires a license by the state, odds are very good that they have a professional society that regulates their members. (See Appendix 7 for a list of state regulated businesses.) You can write to the professional society on your letterhead and ask if Bill is a member in good standing and how long he has been a member. The society will be more than happy to vouch for his standing. The letter you receive back will give his date of membership and may contain some information on his educational background. It will almost certainly contain the date he received his professional license.

You can then write to the state licensing agency and for a fee obtain a copy of his professional license. In some vocations, such as pilots, the federal government maintains the licensing. The federal government will provide you with a copy of the license of any pilot for a fee of a few dollars.

The point of all this is to obtain a rough idea of Bill's qualifications so that we can guess at his salary accurately. Once we know his qualifications and job title, we can send a letter to Bill's company asking what rates of compensation they would pay, let's say, an economist with a Ph.D. and 3 years of experience, exactly Bill's qualifications. On the letter we would say we are doing a salary survey in the Portland area and companies responding will not be named. Send your letter to the personnel office.

If Bill works for any government agency, state or federal, or any institution supported by tax dollars, you can get his salary easily. Taxpayers have a right to know the compensation of employees of the state or local governments. For example, if Bill was a schoolteacher, you could request to see the financial records of the school district, saying that you were an irate taxpayer. If Bill is a university professor, you can find out his rate of pay by searching through the correct indexes at the university library or by writing the state revenue office directly for where to get information. A listing of state tax offices is in Appendix 8. Federal workers' salaries are easily available. Simply call the local office of the General Services Administration and ask what a particular grade of worker would earn.

To get an up-to-the-minute credit status on Bill, you need a copy of his credit report. Right now we have no idea of how deeply in debt Bill is or what his payment history is like. Maybe Bill can make the car payment and the mortgage, but nothing else.

How can we get a copy of Bill's credit report? You can get it one of three ways. The first is to write to the credit bureau in Bill's name, requesting a copy of his credit file. You would provide Bill's name, his birthdate, Social Security number, his last home address, and his "new" home address — your location. You will need to enclose the fee, so call the credit bureau first to find out the current fee. Within two weeks you will have a copy of Bill's credit report.

The second method would involve going into a department store and applying for an "instant" department store credit card. Often you are not required to show any identification. You would do the following. You would tell the salesman that you would like to purchase a color TV on credit. After the sale is written up, he will have you go upstairs to the credit office and fill out a short-form credit application. You already know all of Bill's personal details, so filling out the form is easy. Within two hours your application will be approved or rejected. If it is rejected, you can take a copy of the rejection letter and send it to the credit bureau and they will send you a free copy of your credit report. If the sale is approved, you would change your mind at the last minute and leave the store. In that case, we know Bill has good credit. The problem is we do not have the actual credit report. In this case, I recommend the third method, which is to use one of the independent search firms listed in Appendix 4 to obtain Bill's credit report for you.

8

Specialized
Databanks

These services should be contacted after you have done your initial information search and it has not yielded much data. However, if you know for sure that information is available from one of these sources, then run a check here as soon as possible. In the example of Bill Jones, we did not know much about him. But what if we know that Bill Jones had been in the military, or perhaps was still connected to the military through the Reserves or the National Guard?

Military records are a boon to a person conducting an information search. Under the Federal Government's Freedom of Information Act, most information from a current or former service member's personnel file must be released upon request. The only data that will not be released is the medical history of the service member, details of any classified assignments, and current address and Social Security number.

What will be released to you is a detailed chronological history of the subject's life in the military. The record will detail all locations of duty assignments, when and where the subject was promoted, the subject's place of birth and date of birth, all children and other dependents of the service member, along with much other data. I draw attention to the information on dependents because it will also include the age and names of the children. This can help you determine the birthdate and birthplace of the children, as well as additional data on the subject's unit assignments; these will allow you to compile a whole network of people you can contact through the military to learn more about your subject.

You would accomplish this by making use of the Military Locator service to find these former colleagues and then contact them. Or you could request these other people's military records and contact them that way. The easiest way to obtain more information on a subject via a former colleague is to make use of the service where the Veterans Administration will forward letters on the seeming grounds of a unit reunion. You would know the unit or units your subject had served in from the Military Service file. This information would be sent to the V.A. along with $2.00 for each colleague you wanted the current address of. The V.A. will provide you with the V.A. file number, the regional office handling the case, and the way to have the letter forwarded.

With current or former military members, the starting point is obtaining the current or past service file. Once you have done this you will often have the information you seek. If not, then arrange to have a letter forwarded to get current address data. In general, by the time you have received the military personnel file, you will already have current address and telephone numbers from other sources. There is a sample Military Record request form in Appendix 9 which includes relevant military search addresses.

Criminal records are the next specialized data base that you will want to check out. Most people do not have criminal records, and if they do, they will usually be picked up by the credit bureau and listed on the subject's credit report. There are cases where this may not happen. If our Mr. Jones was convicted of an offense ten years ago, it will no longer appear on his credit report.

Your information search will have given you a chronological history of Bill Jones' addresses. Most cities and counties sell something called a "compliance" certificate or something similar. These certificates say that the person named therein does not have a criminal record with the city or county involved. Frequently companies that require their employees to be bonded require that applicants obtain these certificates before they will be formally hired. Often this can be done by mail by sending in the appropriate fee and request form to the county or city records clerk. You would apply for such a Certificate in the name of the target. If it is issued, you can safely assume that he has no record. You could do this for each locale where he lived.

In some cities there is open access to the criminal litigation index. You can actually sit at a computer terminal and search the index yourself. The litigation index will provide the nature of the charge, the judge and attorneys involved, and the case disposition along with other information. Federal criminal records can also be obtained this way. Although the actual criminal record itself is restricted data, the court proceedings that led to its establishment are not.

Federal court indexes are better organized than local or state court indexes. Essentially, you do the identical procedure, but at the Federal Courts concerned. You might also wish to check at the Federal bankruptcy court as well. Private firms that advertise that they can get a criminal record on an individual essentially do the same thing or they know someone in law enforcement who will run National Crime Information Computer checks for them. You can accomplish the same.

Other specialized databanks to check out are city business license records and the county fictitious name index. Most cities require all businesses to be licensed. If it appears that the company your subject works for may be owned in part by the subject, check out the business license. These are public records. City business license records will usually detail the owner of record, the officers of the business, and the addresses of these people. License renewals will often request data on last year's sales figures, and frequently contain Social Security numbers and business tax identification numbers for all listed parties. The county fictitious names index is an index of private operators who use a "doing business as" name for their operation. These forms will be on record at the county courthouse, and contain a similar amount of data.

Getting medical data on a target can be difficult. However, there are ways to get at least a partial perspective on the target's medical history. The equivalent of a credit bureau for the insurance industry is something called the Medical Information Bureau. For short, it is known as the MIB. The MIB contains the health records of millions of Americans who have health insurance and have made claims against it. The MIB will not give you any information directly, but you can access it without their knowledge. The MIB acts like a credit bureau does to those who have bad credit. Except in this case, "bad credit" is a poor medical history.

People who have been treated for certain serious illnesses find out later on that they can never purchase any more health insurance. The MIB sees to this with ruthless efficiency. Part of an insured person's agreement with the insurer allows a copy of the patient's medical history to be placed on file at the MIB. As claims are made against your insurance, they are logged at the MIB. At some point, you may become a "bad risk." At this point, you will be denied further insurance coverage. An easy way to see if your subject has had any serious medical claims is to apply for a supplemental hospital cash policy in his name. If the policy is granted, odds are his medical history is relatively clean. If you get a letter back from the company saying coverage is denied entirely, or they will grant coverage but will exclude certain illnesses, you can almost bet he has had these. A follow-up letter to the particular carrier involved will often net you a more detailed response about the illness involved.

Finally, I will close with how you can obtain the tax return of the subject. At this point in your search you should know almost every important detail about your subject. All you require to get a copy of his tax return is his name, address, and Social Security number. Write to the IRS to get the request form and find out the correct fee. Mail in the completed form and the fee and the IRS will send you his return. In fact, the request form includes a space for the return to be sent to someone other than the taxpayer concerned!

| 9 |

Conducting a Debtor Search

All searches have one principal guideline: you get as much information as you can without outside help, and only if you are unable to obtain satisfactory results on your own do you turn to a third party. These sources will be discussed later on.

Let's suppose that you are working as an independent investigator and you have been given the file on a John Doe who owes the Acme Finance Company two thousand dollars on a personal loan account. The loan was taken out three years ago and there had been intermittent periods of late payments over this time. About a year ago the payments ceased, and the account went into collection and eventually was charged off. The company's contract collection agency was assigned the account, but with no result. The file you have been given contains the original loan application, copies of the cancelled checks tendered in payment, and an old credit report. We can assume that the easy work was already done. The outside collection agency would have already contacted his local bank, employer and any other creditors or relatives listed on the application. This will have yielded no results. We can assume that our subject has left the area, and has no assets that can be easily traced. Where do you begin?

The first step is to expend a little energy finding out about our target's past. Obviously, the relatives or friends listed on the loan application will not say anything, but how about his former landlord? A quick visit here will often get you some answers about his past. Most importantly, check any references listed on the application. This will give you an idea as to where he came from before he relocated to your area. It will also allow you to talk to his former neighbors to learn more about him. Now we are armed with more information than most collection agencies will even bother to obtain. We now begin the second phase of the search.

People tend to return to places they have come from. You would run an alpha driver record search in your current state, his previous state of residence and all neighboring states. If he had any cars, it is a good idea to do the same thing with respect to his vehicle registrations. In a week's time you should have some idea as to his whereabouts. But you must be able to properly interpret the information you will receive from these sources. For example, if you find that he did not renew his vehicle registration, one of two things happened. The first possibility is that he moved out of state, and re-registered his car there. The second possibility is that he sold the car to someone else. If the purchaser was within your current state, it means that the vehicle has not yet been re-registered, otherwise the computer will show that the registration has been transferred to the new owner. If the car has been sold to an out-of-state buyer, the computer will not show this. This is because most states, after checking to see that the car is not stolen, simply issue new plates and registration, and shred the old documents. Your multi-state search will give you an answer if he has a drivers license or car registered in any of these states.

The most wide-reaching vehicle search you can run is called a vehicle identification number search, or VIN search, for short. This works if the subject has changed his name and registered the car to himself in this new name. The VIN of a car will never change. This is the unique serial number that the manufacturer gives every car or truck at the factory. A VIN search will give you the name and address of the legal and registered owner. If he has sold the car, the VIN search will tell you that at once. For this reason, you may prefer to run a VIN search at once instead of an alpha search. But remember, to run a VIN search you must first have the serial number.

The next angle to work is to see if he has left a forwarding address anywhere. You would, of course, have already asked the former landlord and neighbors if they had a new address. If nothing was forthcoming, you can assume that he did not tell anyone where he would be. However, most people want to get their mail, and he may have filed an address change form with the Post Office. All change of address forms can be obtained in one of two manners. The first involves a Freedom of Information Act request. If you file this request form the Post Office must tell you who the boxholder is, or what the forwarding address is. This leads us naturally to the second source of data, which is a third party information broker.

The Post Office sells off the listing of all address changes to a number of information vendors. You can always obtain this list of address changes from them. I will explain more about this later, but you may be wondering why I take the attitude I do toward the use of third party information vendors.

There is a place for using these services in a search. But you should only use these sources when you have already exhausted your own efforts. It is especially bad practice to develop a heavy reliance on these sources as a beginning investigator, because you will never develop the tracking skills a good investigator must have.

Back to our debtor search. While you are waiting for a response on your motor vehicle and address forwarding records, now is the time to start working some other angles. One is to contact the telephone company. If he has skipped out on other bills, there is a good chance that he stiffed the phone company on the last bill as well. Often telephone company collections agents will be willing to share some information with you if you agree to tell them about any additional information your investigation turns up. Make sure you follow through, even if it is just to say that you have nothing new to report. Sometimes you can obtain a listing of long distance numbers that the subject has called. This can put you on track when it seems like an investigation is deadending. This can also lead your search to a state where you had not considered running a check of the records before. Sometimes talking with the person whom he has called will elicit information as to your target's whereabouts. Often you will have to use a cover story. This is known as pretexting. You must use some care when doing so, however. Never, ever pretend you are a doctor or a lawyer or a police officer or other professional person. You can get into serious trouble for doing that. You can get away with such ruses as saying that you have an urgent message for the target, or that he has some unclaimed property due him, and those who have it need to know his current address. Another excellent pretext is to say that the subject has listed you as a personal reference in connection with an employment application. You can easily maneuver the conversation around so you can obtain some current address information.

Let's say that you have gone through all of these steps and you still have been unable to locate your subject. This is when you would turn to a third party information broker. For example, to run a fifty state search of motor vehicle records would be very costly. A third party information provider can do this. One way is through the credit bureau header information mentioned previously. If you know the subject's name, Social Security number and birthdate, you can use these services effectively.

One company that purchases access to this header data from all of the credit bureaus on a nationwide basis is called IRSC. Another company that provides this service is called NCI, for National Credit Information. Both of these networks also incorporate other databases such as change of address records and nationwide Criss-Cross directory capability. These services can be accessed in one of two ways. Either online through computer, or by telephone or mail.

With these services you establish an account that entitles you to so many searches. As this book is not an advertisement for these companies, prices can be had by writing to them at the addresses in Appendix 4. Let's look at how an online search would work.

When you use these services you are given a choice as to information sources. The first source offered will usually be the one that can give the most accurate information. Credit bureau files are generally the best source. If no match is made, the system will direct you to the next best source of information. There are online databases that will allow you to run almost any type of search.

10

Conducting Background Investigations

Background investigations are another potential source of revenue for an investigator. Most background investigations are what is known as a passive investigation.

Consider what happens when a company wants a bonded employee. Before the insurance company will agree to bond a company's employees, it will first want some type of assurance that the workers have no criminal record, for theft in particular. All criminal records are public information. The investigation that will follow will usually involve no more than checking out the criminal litigation index in the counties or cities that the applicant has lived in. If the search is negative, meaning that there are no criminal records on file for this individual, then the bond will be issued.

This sort of work is easy. Many smaller businesses now want to do some type of pre-employment screening of all their employees, for liability purposes. The thing to bear in mind with criminal records is that the only thing that is privileged about them is the mode of access. All states have a central criminal records computer repository, as does the FBI on a national level. This database is off limits unless you know someone in law enforcement who has access. The federal system is called the National Crime Information Computer. This is the one that police officers routinely use when they pull someone over and check the person out. The other part of these records is the criminal record index. This is a separate listing of all people who have been convicted of serious criminal offenses in the United States.

One way to have access to these records on a nationwide basis is to use the services of one of the aforementioned third party search firms. The way these firms work is they have someone in every county who can physically check the criminal files in that locale. Some of these companies actually maintain their own parallel computerized database of criminal records. Once again, use these services only when necessary. If you run criminal history checks in a few locales all the time, you will know what the current fee and request form is.

Another nationwide source of data is licensing bodies and professional associations. If you know a person works in a trade or profession that normally requires licensing or union membership, you have a ready-made access to information. A letter or telephone call to the licensing agency will tell you if the person is working in that particular state. These organizations are normally only too happy to provide information, because this allows them to protect their membership from unlicensed competitors. A listing of state regulated occupations is given in Appendix 7.

State licensing bodies can be very useful in doing another type of investigative work. Universities and colleges of all sorts need to stay in touch with their alumni for fundraising purposes. As the federal government has cut back on education funding, this type of contact has become more vital. Because many university and college graduates practice or work in state regulated industries, locating these people just boils down to identifying the current state of residence, and then contacting the relevant professional association or state licensing body.

This brings us to a special case of people who have been in the military. Military records should not be overlooked as a potential source of information, even if it has been many years since the person was in the Armed Forces. All military personnel and service records are universally available to anyone. This is due to the fact that military people are paid with public funds.

Military service records will tell all about a former or current service member's personal and military life. These records contain such data as family members' names and birthdates, and whether or not the serviceman is married or has children. The duty side of the records will contain such information as the date of enlistment, or in the case of officers, the date of commissioning, all active duty assignments, the pay received, and the time in grade or rank, and promotion history. Active-duty service members can be located quickly through a service known as the Armed Services Locator service. The reserve components and national guard also have similar locator services.

Another valuable source of information is the county real estate index. This is arranged alphabetically by the last names of all people buying and selling property during the year. This is a public record document and is available without the need for doing any pretexting at all. These records will tell who the seller was, how much was paid for the property, and the name of the mortgage holder, if any. This can provide valuable leads on a person and with whom they have had financial dealings. This can provide an avenue to learn about such things as income and assets.

Passive vs. Active Investigations

All investigations have the same goal. That goal is to expose various aspects of a person's life that are of interest. An investigation can take different forms. When a person applies for a new job and is asked to give references from his last employment, this is a background investigation. Background investigations can be divided into two types. These are passive investigations and active investigations.

A passive investigation is the kind most of us are familiar with. In a passive investigation, the lack of any negative information is considered proof positive that the individual concerned is worthy of the job or other privilege to be granted. An active investigation is a horse of a completely different color. The active investigator is not satisfied with the mere lack of negative information. The investigator actively seeks out discrepancies in an individual's story or background, and upon finding them, tries to expose as much detail about them as possible. Consider the difference in how educational credentials would be verified in a passive investigation and an active one.

Assume that we are conducting a passive investigation of an individual. This individual has applied for a job that requires a university degree. On the resume, the job applicant has written that he has a degree and also what his grade point average was. The passive investigator will simply call the university in question to confirm the degree and the grade point average. On hearing confirmation of this, the passive investigator will regard the matter as being closed and move onto something else.

The active investigator takes an entirely different approach. The active investigator will not be content with merely obtaining confirmation of the individual's educational bona fides. He will write and obtain the actual transcript and student record. With these, he will look carefully at the courses taken and at the specific grades received to see if there is anything there that was not listed on the resume.

Active investigating got a big boost in the 1980s after the major spy case involving the Walker family. In 1985, four members of this family were convicted of engaging in espionage against the United States. The secrets they betrayed dealt with the nuclear missile firing submarines, in particular the coding system used to issue missile launch orders. The members of this family had all passed traditional passive background investigations conducted by the military. After this incident, and others around the same time, the whole business of background investigations was revamped.

It was decided that the passive investigations that had been done up to this point were no longer adequate, and that the active investigations that previously had only been done on applicants at the highest levels would be extended to almost all Defense Department security clearance investigations. The new system would be similar to the British system called "positive vetting." In these types of investigations it is virtually impossible for an individual to slip through the net undetected.

We will first look at how passive investigations are carried out. This is due to the fact that most private company investigations, state-level clearances and federal civil service investigations are done in this fashion.

Passive Investigations

When you see a job that says "background investigation required" advertised by a state agency, federal civil service or private employer, it will usually involve a passive investigation. This investigation will involve two parts. The first will be verification of an applicant's employment and educational background. The second will involve checking certain databases for negative information. Perhaps the most familiar type of passive investigation that goes on is when a person is bonded for certain types of employment. This is very common in the banking and janitorial businesses. An insurance company agrees to indemnify the business in question, provided all employees meet their screening requirements. People often wonder what happens if a bank teller gives out ten one-hundred-dollar bills instead of ten ten-dollar bills. The teller might be fired, but the insurance company pays the losses.

Bonding requirements are usually quite simple. They normally only require that the applicant have no criminal record. Such things as traffic infractions are not considered, unless it is drunk driving. Quite often the applicant himself is required to go to the local police and obtain a certificate of good character. This is a simple passive investigation.

Some passive investigations can be more encompassing than this. The one thing all passive investigations have in common is that the databases that are consulted will only contain information on the exceptional citizen. A good example is the background investigation of a person who wants to drive trucks in interstate transportation of merchandise. Most trucking companies will do a passive investigation that is more comprehensive than just a simple bonding check. The trucking company needs to know that the driver is not prone to steal from his shipments, that his driving record is not riddled with accidents, and that his licenses are valid and he possesses the necessary background. This can all be accomplished through a passive investigation.

The databases that must be consulted are many. Let's look at the driving history first. The investigator will want to contact the Motor Vehicle Department of the state where he was issued his Commercial Driving License. His driving record will tell whether or not his license is valid, and also his entire driving history. All traffic citations and accidents will be listed. This will tell if the applicant has given a true picture of his driving background. Once it has been determined that the driving history meets the company's requirements, the investigator can proceed with the next step in verifying his background. This will involve a criminal background check. The investigator will write to the court clerks in each state and city of residence asking them to search for a criminal record in the name of this individual. If the result is negative, the investigator will then proceed with verifying the employment and educational background of the applicant. This will usually involve no more than making a few telephone calls to former employers and asking if the applicant worked there in the capacities given and also ascertaining what type of worker he is.

If all of these checks are negative, meaning no derogatory information is found, the applicant has successfully passed this passive investigation, and he will be hired.

Passive investigations all share certain common features. The most important one is that a lack of negative information from certain sources is considered positive and serves to validate the background claimed.

To aid passive investigations, many states are creating new databases. One example involves medical doctors. Many of the states, with the help of the federal government, are compiling a nationwide database of all medical practitioners whose licenses have been suspended, revoked, or found guilty of malpractice claims. This database will provide an easy way to check if a doctor has been the subject of such adverse action. When the system is complete, an investigator would merely input the name, birthdate and Social Security number of the doctor in question, and the system would respond with either a no or yes.

Over time, many agencies will come to rely on this system, in passive investigations, as the arbiter of a doctor's standing. But one example of how these databases can give a false sense of security is one of the oldest, the National Drivers Register. Almost every state uses it, and it is an example of how "negative information" databases do not always work reliably.

The National Drivers Registry is supposed to contain the names and birthdates of every driver in the United States who has had a license revoked, or is currently under suspension. When a person applies for a new driving license in most states, this database is automatically consulted on line by the computer. If the National Driver Register indicates that the new license applicant has a file, the new license application will be denied. The applicant will be told that he must resolve the existing problem before any new license can be issued. The National Driver Register is designed to catch drivers who make simple attempts to evade it, such as transposing their first and middle names. However, a negative database like this can very easily be defeated. If a person transposes their first and middle names, and gives a different Social Security number, the system is easily defeated.

Almost all negative databases can be easily outmaneuvered in a similar fashion. For example, some states have a computerized listing of all people suspected of child sexual abuse. If a person gets on one of these lists, even when it occurs with no evidence, it is virtually impossible to get off of the list. People whose names are wrongly on these lists find they cannot work in a whole range of jobs, because they might have some contact with children.

However, such computerized blacklisting can be overcome by simply altering enough personal data so that it does not match the information contained on the list. A person who is on a state child abuser list can change the order of his names and his Social Security number and eliminate his problems.

Because negative databases can be evaded in this way, an investigator may wish to check out transposed versions of the name the subject is using. This can expose people using this simple method to hide negative information. But to reveal negative information about someone who has used more elaborate methods of creating a new identity requires an active background investigation, as described later in this chapter.

Let's look at the databases that are typically consulted in a passive investigation and how they operate.

One of the most consulted databases is the credit bureau network across the country. In most states, it is perfectly legal for an employer to order a credit bureau report on a job applicant. Quite often in the small print on job applications, a waiver is given allowing the employer to do just that. In general, the only employers who will bother with credit checks are those where the employee's job will involve contact with cash or valuables. The logic is that someone with bad credit and in debt up to their ears will not make an employee who can be trusted. Some employers regard good credit as a sign of reliability. Once again, what is being looked for is the finding of negative information.

The next major database checked will be the county criminal record index. As we saw earlier, employers that require bonding of employees will always check this. They will also check in the counties where the applicant previously resided. All county courts will provide the record, or non-record of a person to anyone who will pay the required fee. Along with these criminal record checks are the other databases that we mentioned before that deal with child molesters and the like. Quite often these checks will be done in tandem.

Motor Vehicle Department records are also readily consulted. Nearly every person has some contact with this department. A person's driving record can be of legitimate interest to any employer who will have company vehicles driven by employees. This database can also be accessed in all states by anyone for payment of a small fee. The National Drivers Register, as previously mentioned, will also be consulted in tandem.

Other databases are the credit bureau networks maintained across the country. In conjunction with these, some investigators will check the county civil litigation index to see if a person is the subject of lawsuits. If a person is the practitioner of a profession or trade that must be licensed, the records of the relevant state licensing body can be consulted.

We should look at the differences between passive investigations conducted by governmental agencies and private corporations. The main difference is in the data banks they are allowed entry to. For example, all states have a criminal identification bureau database in the state capital. Ordinarily this is only available to law enforcement officers, and private individuals and companies are not allowed access to it. The state criminal identification bureau compiles its data from the local counties. Whenever a person is arrested on a serious charge, the fingerprint data and charge disposition sheet are forwarded to the bureau. The FBI criminal record index is in turn compiled from the files in the state identification bureau.

Some state and most Federal governmental agencies that run passive background investigations on individuals are able to access these databases directly. In fact, this is often called a "National Agency Check" when a passive investigation is done in this fashion. What needs to be realized is that there is no different information available here. Only the method of access is different. Instead of checking each former county of residence for the existence of a record, one goes directly to the state identification bureau. We should also mention that many quasi-governmental bodies such as school boards also have access to these types of databases. If a private investigator has a friend who works in law enforcement, for example, he may be able to take a short cut in obtaining certain information.

Active Investigations

The active investigation proceeds in a totally different manner than the passive background investigation. This concept became very popular in Great Britain years ago. It is called "positive vetting."

An active background investigation pursued to its furthest ends should be able to reveal every significant event in a person's life, from their birth to the present. In effect, this is what active investigations of the highest order attempt to do. This also exposes the inherent weakness of the passive investigation. The passive investigator relies upon databases that will only contain information on the exceptional citizen. The other tool the active background investigation utilizes is time-line techniques. With these techniques, a chart can be plotted that shows a person's movement through each phase of his life. A person who passes such an investigation can be said to have few secrets left.

Another key aspect of active investigation techniques is periodic reevaluation of the subject. People who interact with the subject presently are interviewed, and an updated search is made on certain databases for new negative information. This type of active investigation would have exposed the Walker family spy ring long before the worst damage was done.

I am going to show how the federal government carries out active background investigations of people who must have a security clearance to work in sensitive positions in the government or the defense industry. This will show you the nature of an active investigation of the highest order, even though it may be a bigger project than you want to tackle.

The beginning of this type of background investigation is the personal history statement. This is a long stack of forms that interrogates the subject about various aspects of his life. The subject must complete these forms at the office, and is not allowed to take them home. The reason for this is that these forms act as a control standard against what the investigation yields. There will be some discrepancies — a person cannot recall exactly every major activity they have done in the last ten years. However, there should not be major differences. One form will ask the subject to detail his educational history since grammar school. Another form will ask him to detail his employment history since he's been an adult. A separate biographical data form will ask him to list his birthdate, birthplace, parental birthdates and birthplaces, as well as other information on his siblings and friends he has known over the years.

Another sheet will ask the subject to detail his financial history over the years. Where he has banked, what credit cards he has, how much money he has in various accounts, and if he has any foreign bank accounts. Another form will ask about his foreign travels and residences. If he has a passport, they will want a photocopy of it. The subject will also have to submit to a fingerprint check, and finally agree to allow his medical records to be examined.

The personal history statement provides the rough data that the investigating agent works with. In the federal government, the FBI is the agency responsible for carrying out the actual investigation. The starting point is a passive investigation of sorts. The subject's fingerprints and personal data will be subjected to a national agency check. The FBI will check them against its own criminal records index, and those of any foreign countries that the subject has visited or lived in. They will also check his name against listings of illegal tax protesters maintained by the Internal Revenue Service. Other agencies' listings of persons of interest are also consulted.

Once this has been completed the field investigation begins. This is where the investigation shifts from a passive to an active mode. At this point in the investigation we can say that the subject is not on the top ten most wanted list and that he has no criminal background. This is what he is not. The objective of the active investigation is to establish who he really is.

The active investigation will start with the details of the subject's birth. The field agent will pay a visit to the state vital statistics bureau and the registrar in the subject's county of birth. These records will be compared with the copy of his birth certificate that he previously provided. The agent will note the small details on the subject's birth certificate. He will jot down if he has any brothers or sisters, where the birth took place, and the name of the attending physician, nurse or midwife. The names of these people will be written down. The agent will also note the name on the subject's birth certificate and notice if there are any variations between the name he uses presently and the name he was given at birth.

The next level of verification that will take place on the subject's birth certificate is to contact the state medical board that licensed whomever the attendant at birth was. They will attempt to verify that the doctor or nurse listed on the certificate actually existed. They will also attempt to contact this person to see if their personal records agree with the birth certificate. The final check involves establishing that any siblings listed exist and that they agree they have a brother or sister of that name.

This may seem to be a lot of trouble to go through for a birth certificate, but when the procedure is finished, there can be no doubt left as to the authenticity of the document. Sometimes a false birth certificate can be put into the files of the county registrar and at the state vital statistics agency. But a false birth certificate will not have generated the secondary records that accompany a real one.

The next step in the active phase of the investigation is to verify the background segment of the personal history statement. This is the sheet where the subject lists his addresses and residences since he was a child. This information will be confirmed in a variety of ways. No, they do not interview all of the subject's old teachers. They will contact the schools listed and check for his attendance during the years indicated. They will also obtain a copy of his transcripts from his high school years and from any schooling above the high school level. These will be compared with ones that are already in his personnel file.

The other way the subject's former residences will be checked is through older editions of the city directories. These are available to the field agents in the various cities where he had lived. They will look under his name, and if he was a child during the years in question, they will look under his family name. When these listings all come back with information substantially verifying the information he provided on the personal history statement, this phase of the active investigation is closed.

At this point, the background investigator can conclude that the subject is the person that he has claimed to be on his personal history statement. His whereabouts for the last ten years are known, and from the day of his birth he has been scrutinized. The second part of the background investigation will involve taking a detailed look at his financial background and status.

The government will order credit reports on the subject from all of the major credit bureaus. They will also contact his bank and other financial institutions. His investment portfolio will be examined to see if it is in line with his income. His credit report will be pored over to see if he is a person who lives within his means, or if he is steadily going deeper and deeper into debt. This is of concern because a person in perilous financial condition can be more easily compromised.

Once his finances have been checked, his medical records will be examined. In his medical file they will look at his overall health over the years and if he has been treated for any medical conditions that indicate certain behaviors. For example, a person who has a history of liver problems may be an alcoholic. What they are searching for is a medical condition that a foreign intelligence agency could use against the subject. If nothing is turned up here, the field investigation moves into its final phase.

The final phase of the background investigation will involve personal interviews with friends and acquaintances who have known the subject over the years. On the personal history statement, he will be asked to provide the names, addresses and telephone numbers of many people who have known him. But these people will be subjected to a background check themselves. This consists of a national agency check to ensure that the people he has listed as references are not criminals. Then the FBI will conduct casual interviews with many of these people and former neighbors.

During these interviews, the government will seek to determine what type of lifestyle the subject has now and has had in the past. This is the most subjective part of the interview process. The government will seek to determine if he fools around on his wife, if he is married, or if he is a closet homosexual, if he is single. They will seek to determine if he engages in such activities as wife swapping and sexual swinging. The reason for this is all of these things can be used to blackmail a person. A person's being a homosexual or bisexual will not automatically disqualify them from receiving a security clearance. It is only if they are still in the closet about these activities. There are many thousands of openly homosexual people who hold security clearances.

A good example of what will cause problems is the case of John Tower, who was nominated to become secretary of defense in 1989 by President George Bush. He had previously been married for many years, and one of the grounds for his divorce had been adultery.

He was also said to have been seen intoxicated in public. As the FBI continued the background investigation, the allegations became more and more numerous. In the end the nomination was rejected by the Senate. Tower's real problem was that he gave the appearance of being an unreliable, undisciplined person through his overall behavior.

One former neighbor who disliked the subject is not enough to kill a background clearance. It is the overall lifestyle that a person has. In effect, what the investigators are looking for is a "smoking gun" that could be used to compromise the subject in the future. Only active investigations are able to ferret out such details. Many people fail these investigations because of a smoking gun in their past. Many people have been successfully turned into agents for hostile nations because the other side identified such Achilles' heels. In fact, a few years ago in California, the Soviet Government attempted to purchase a bank that served many people who held top secret security clearances and worked at a sensitive military electronics plant. The Soviets were thwarted at the last minute. Clearly they were hoping to find some employees who were in trouble financially and could be compromised.

When the field investigation is completed the results are given to the agent in charge of the investigation. He then makes a recommendation as to whether the clearance should be granted or denied. Generally this decision can be appealed by the subject of the investigation.

Depending on the situation, a private investigator may not be able to use all the techniques the federal government uses to carry out an active background investigation of an individual. For example, it may not be feasible, in some cases, to have the subject fill out a personal history statement. This will obviously make things harder for the investigator, who will have to take whatever information he has about the subject and use the various data sources discussed earlier in this book to build up a more complete picture of the subject's background. This will provide the investigator with the leads he needs, such as the names of family members of the subject, as a starting point for an active background investigation.

Appendix 1

Sample Worksheet

Full Name: _____

Variants of First Name/Nicknames: _____

Date of Birth: _____

Social Security Number: _____

Current Address: _____

Former Address: _____

Telephone: _____

Marital Status/Spouse's Name: _____

Present Employer: _____

Job Title: _____

Years of Service: _____Salary: _____

Landlord Address: _____

Mortgage Holder: _____

Car Registrations: _____

Driver License Number: _____

Military Service Record:_____

Criminal Record History:

   Local:_____

   Federal: _____

Medical Record:_____

Place of Birth: _____

Educational Background: _____

Credit Bureau File:_____

Appendix $\boxed{2}$

State
Motor Vehicle
Department Offices

ALABAMA
Department of Public Safety
Drivers License Division
P.O. Box 1471
Montgomery, AL 36192   (205) 261-4400

ALASKA
Department of Public Safety
Pouch N
Juneau, AK 99811   (907) 465-4364

ARIZONA
Motor Vehicle Division
1801 West Jefferson
Phoenix, AZ 85009   (602) 255-7723

ARKANSAS
Office of Driver Services
P.O. Box 1272
Little Rock, AR 72203   (501) 371-1743

CALIFORNIA
Department of Motor Vehicles
Division of Drivers Licenses
P.O. Box 12590
Sacramento, CA 95813   (916) 445-6236

COLORADO
Motor Vehicle Division
140 West 6th Avenue
Denver, CO 80204   (303) 866-3407

CONNECTICUT
Department of Motor Vehicles
60 State Street
Wethersfield, CT 06109   (203) 566-3300

DELAWARE
Motor Vehicle Division
P.O. Box 698
Highway Administration Building
Dover, DE 19901   (302) 736-4497

DISTRICT OF COLUMBIA
Department of Motor Vehicles
301 C Street N.W.
Washington, DC 20001   (202) 727-6679

FLORIDA
Division of Drivers Licenses
Department of Highway Safety
Neil Kirkman Building
Tallahassee, FL 32301   (904) 488-3144

GEORGIA
Department of Public Safety
P.O. Box 1456
Atlanta, GA 30371   (404) 656-5890

HAWAII
Motor Vehicle Safety Office
Department of Transportation
869 Punchbowl Street
Honolulu, HI 96813   (808) 548-3205/5756

IDAHO
Motor Vehicle Bureau
P.O. Box 34
Boise, ID 83731   (208) 334-2586

ILLINOIS
Department of Motor Vehicles
2701 Dirksen Parkway
Springfield, IL 62723   (217) 782-6212

INDIANA
Bureau of Motor Vehicles
State Office Building, Room 4021
Indianapolis, IN 46204   (317) 232-2798

IOWA
Department of Transportation
Office of Drivers License
Lucas Office Building
Des Moines, IA 50319   (515) 281-5649

KANSAS
Department of Revenue
Division of Vehicles
State Office Building
Topeka, KS 66626   (913) 296-3601

KENTUCKY
Transportation Cabinet
Division of Drivers Licensing
State Office Building
Frankfort, KY 40622   (502) 564-6800

LOUISIANA
Department of Public Safety
Office of Motor Vehicles
P.O. Box 64886
Baton Rouge, LA 70896   (504) 925-6343

MAINE
Secretary of State
Division of Motor Vehicles
Augusta, ME 04333   (207) 289-3585

MARYLAND
Motor Vehicle Administration
6601 Ritchie Highway
Glen Burnie, MD 21062   (301) 768-7255

MASSACHUSETTS
Registry of Motor Vehicles
100 Nashua Street
Boston, MA 02114   (617) 727-3700

MICHIGAN
Bureau of Driver & Vehicle Records
Secondary Complex
Lansing, MI 48918   (517) 322-1460

MINNESOTA
Drivers License Division
161 Transportation Building
St. Paul, MN 55155   (612) 296-6000

MISSISSIPPI
   Department of Public Safety
   P.O. Box 958
   Jackson, MS 39205   (601) 982-1212

MISSOURI
   Drivers License Bureau
   P.O. Box 200
   Jefferson City, MO 65101   (314) 751-2733

MONTANA
   Drivers Services
   303 North Roberts
   Helena, MT 59620   (406) 444-3273

NEBRASKA
   Department of Motor Vehicles
   301 Centennial Mall South
   P.O. Box 94789
   Lincoln, NE 65809   (402) 471-2281

NEVADA
   Department of Motor Vehicles
   Drivers License Division
   555 Wright Way
   Carson City, NV 89711   (702) 885-5360

NEW HAMPSHIRE
   Division of Motor Vehicles
   Hazen Drive
   Concord, NH 03301   (603) 271-2371

NEW JERSEY
   Division of Motor Vehicles
   25 South Montgomery Street
   Trenton, NJ 08666   (609) 292-9849

NEW MEXICO
Motor Vehicle Division
Drivers Service Bureau
Manuel Lujan Sr. Building
Santa Fe, NM 87503   (505) 827-2362

NEW YORK
License Production Bureau
P.O. Box 2688
Empire Plaza
Albany, NY 12220   (518) 474-2068

NORTH CAROLINA
Division of Motor Vehicles
1100 New Bern Avenue
Raleigh, NC 27697   (919) 733-4241

NORTH DAKOTA
State License Division
State Highway Building
Capitol Grounds
Bismarck, ND 58505   (701) 224-4353

OHIO
Bureau of Motor Vehicles
4300 Kimberly Parkway
Columbus, OH 43227   (614) 466-7666

OKLAHOMA
Department of Public Safety
3600 North Eastern
Oklahoma City, OK 73136   (405) 424-0411

OREGON
Motor Vehicle Division
1905 Lana Avenue N.E.
Salem, OR 97301   (503) 378-6994

PENNSYLVANIA
Bureau of Driver Licensing
Commonwealth & Forster
Harrisburg, PA 17122   (717) 787-3130

RHODE ISLAND
Division of Motor Vehicles
State Office Building
Providence, RI 02903   (401) 277-3000

SOUTH CAROLINA
Department of Highways & Public Transportation
Motor Vehicle Division
Drawer 1498
Columbia, SC 29216   (803) 758-3201

SOUTH DAKOTA
Department of Public Safety
118 West Capitol
Pierre, SD 57501   (605) 773-3191

TENNESSEE
Department of Safety
Andrew Jackson State Office Building
Nashville, TN 37210

TEXAS
Department of Public Safety
P.O. Box 4087
5805 North Lamar
Austin, TX 78773   (512) 465-2000

UTAH
Department of Public Safety
Drivers License Division
4501 South 2700 West
Salt Lake City, UT 84119   (801) 965-4400

VERMONT
Department of Motor Vehicles
Montpelier, VT 05602   (802) 828-2121

VIRGINIA
Department of Motor Vehicles
P.O. Box 27412
Richmond, VA 23269-0001   (804) 257-0406

WASHINGTON
Department of Licensing
Highways-Licenses Building
Olympia, WA 98504   (206) 753-6977

WEST VIRGINIA
Department of Motor Vehicles
1800 Washington Street East
Charleston, WV 25317   (304) 348-2719

WISCONSIN
Division of Motor Vehicles
4802 Sheboygan Avenue
Madison, WI 53702   (608) 266-2237

WYOMING
Motor Vehicle Division
2200 Carey Avenue
Cheyenne, WY 82002   (307) 777-7971

Appendix 3

Social Security Number List

Alabama	416-424	Michigan	362-386
Alaska	574	Minnesota	468-477
Arizona	526-527	Mississippi	425-428
Arkansas	429-432	Missouri	486-500
California	545-573	Montana	516-517
Colorado	521-524	Nebraska	505-508
Connecticut	040-049	Nevada	530
Delaware	221-222	New Hampshire	001-003
D.C.	577-579	New Jersey	135-158
Florida	261-267	New Mexico	525 & 585
Georgia	252-260	New York	050-134
Hawaii	575-576	North Carolina	237-246
Idaho	518-519	North Dakota	501-502
Illinois	318-361	Ohio	268-302
Indiana	303-317	Oklahoma	440-448
Iowa	478-485	Oregon	540-544
Kansas	509-515	Pennsylvania	159-211
Kentucky	400-407	Rhode Island	035-039
Louisiana	433-439	South Carolina	247-251
Maine	004-007	South Dakota	503-504
Maryland	212-220	Tennessee	408-415
Massachusetts	010-034	Texas	449-467

Utah	528-529
Vermont	008-009
Virginia	223-231
Washington	531-539
West Virginia	223-231
Wisconsin	387-399
Wyoming	520

Additions

Arizona	600-601
California	602-626
Florida	589-595
Mississippi	587-588
New Mexico	585
North Carolina	232

Miscellaneous

Virgin Islands	580
Puerto Rico	580-584
Guam, Samoa & Pacific Terr.	586
Railroad Ret.	700-728

Appendix | 4 |

Independent
Search
Firms

International Research Service
3777 North Harbor Blvd.
Fullerton, CA 92635

VOS
P.O. Box 15334
Sacramento, CA 95851

Data Search
3600 American River Dr.
Sacramento, CA 95825

The Nationwide Locator
P.O. Box 39903
San Antonio, TX 78218

People Searching News
P.O. Box 22611
Fort Lauderdale, FL 33335

Appendix ⬛ 5

Directory of
Highway Patrol
Accident Reports

ALABAMA
Department of Public Safety
Highway Patrol Division
P.O. Box 1511
Montgomery, AL 36192   (205) 271-4393

ALASKA
Department of Public Safety
Pouch N
Juneau, AK 99811   (907) 465-4363

ARIZONA
Department of Public Safety
2010 West Encanto Boulevard
Phoenix, AZ 85005   (602) 262-8011

ARKANSAS
Department of Public Safety
P.O. Box 4005
Little Rock, AR 72204   (501) 371-2491

CALIFORNIA
California Highway Patrol
2611 26th Street
Sacramento, CA 95814   (916) 445-7473

COLORADO
Colorado State Patrol
4201 East Arkansas Avenue
Denver, CO 80222   (303) 757-9011

CONNECTICUT
State Police Department
100 Washington Street
Hartford, CT 06101   (203) 566-3200

DELAWARE
Division of State Police
P.O. Box 430
Dover, DE 19901   (302) 736-5973

DISTRICT OF COLUMBIA
Washington Metro Police
300 Indiana Avenue N.W.
Washington, DC 20001   (202) 626-2000

FLORIDA
Florida Highway Patrol
Neil Kirkman Building
Tallahassee, FL 32301   (904) 488-6517

GEORGIA
Georgia State Patrol
P.O. Box 1456
Atlanta, GA 30371   (404) 656-6063

HAWAII-HAWAII COUNTY
Police Department
P.O. Box 787
349 Kapiolani Street
Hilo, HI 96720   (808) 961-2211

HAWAII-HONOLULU COUNTY
Department of Finance
Division of Motor Vehicles & Licensing
1455 South Beretania Street
Honolulu, HI 96814   (808) 943-3428

HAWAII-KAUAI COUNTY
Police Department
3060 Umi Street
Lehue, HI 96766   (808) 245-6721

HAWAII-MAUI COUNTY
Police Department
Wailuku, HI 96793   (808) 244-7811

IDAHO
Transportation Department
3311 West State Street
Boise, ID 83703   (208) 334-3664

ILLINOIS
Illinois State Police
401 Armory
Springfield, IL 62706   (217) 782-2841

INDIANA
Indiana State Police
State Office Building, Room 301
100 North Senate Avenue
Indianapolis, IN 46204   (317) 232-8241

IOWA
Iowa State Patrol
Department of Public Safety
Lucas State Office Building
Des Moines, IA 50319 (515) 281-5824

KANSAS
Kansas Highway Patrol
200 East 6th Street
Topeka, KS 66603 (913) 296-3801

KENTUCKY
Justice Cabinet
State Police Headquarters
919 Versailles Road
Frankfort, KY 40601 (502) 695-6300

LOUISIANA
State Police
65 South Foster Drive
P.O. Box 66614
Baton Rouge, LA 70896 (504) 925-6006

MAINE
State Police
36 Hospital Street
Augusta, ME 04330 (207) 289-3111

MARYLAND
State Police
Pikesville, MD 21208 (301) 486-3101

MASSACHUSETTS
Division of State Police
1010 Commonwealth Avenue
Boston, MA 02115 (617) 566-4500

MICHIGAN
Department of State Police
714 South Harrison Road
East Lansing, MI 48823   (517) 332-2521

MINNESOTA
Department of Public Safety
211 Highway Building
St. Paul, MN 55155   (612) 296-6642

MISSISSIPPI
Department of Public Safety
Highway Patrol
P.O. Box 958
Jackson, MS 39205   (601) 982-1212

MISSOURI
State Highway Patrol
1510 East Elm Street
Jefferson City, MO 65101   (314) 751-3313

MONTANA
Highway Patrol Division
303 North Roberts
Helena, MT 59620   (406) 444-3000

NEBRASKA
State Patrol
State House Station
P.O. Box 94907
Lincoln, NE 65809   (402) 471-4545

NEVADA
Department of Motor Vehicles
Highway Patrol Division
555 Wright Way
Carson City, NV 89711   (702) 885-5300

NEW HAMPSHIRE
State Police
Hazen Drive
Concord, NH 03301   (603) 271-3636

NEW JERSEY
Division of Motor Vehicles
25 South Montgomery Street
Trenton, NJ 08666   (609) 292-9849

NEW MEXICO
State Police
P.O. Box 1628
Santa Fe, NM 87503   (505) 827-5111

NEW YORK
Division of State Police
Building 22, State Campus
Albany, NY 12226   (518) 457-6721

NORTH CAROLINA
Highway Patrol
P.O. Box 27687
Archdale Building
Raleigh, NC 27611   (919) 829-7952

NORTH DAKOTA
Highway Patrol
Capitol Grounds
Bismarck, ND 58505   (701) 224-2455

OHIO
State Highway Patrol
660 East Main Street
Columbus, OH 43205   (614) 466-2300

OKLAHOMA
Highway Patrol
3600 North Eastern
Oklahoma City, OK 73136   (405) 424-4011

OREGON
State Police
1905 Lana Avenue N.E.
Salem, OR 97301   (503) 378-3720

PENNSYLVANIA
State Police
1800 Elmerton Avenue
Harrisburg, PA 17109   (717) 787-5517

RHODE ISLAND
State Police
P.O. Box 185
North Scituate, RI 02857   (401) 647-3311

SOUTH CAROLINA
Law Enforcement Division
955 Park Street
Columbia, SC 29201   (803) 758-3315

SOUTH DAKOTA
Division of Highway Patrol
118 West Capitol
Pierre, SD 57501   (605) 773-3105

TENNESSEE
Highway Patrol
1226 Andrew Jackson
 State Office Building
Nashville, TN 37219   (615) 741-2925

TEXAS
Highway Patrol
P.O. Box 4087
5805 North Lamar
Austin, TX 78773   (512) 465-2000

UTAH
Highway Patrol
4501 South 2700 W.
Salt Lake City, UT 84419   (801) 965-4549

VERMONT
Department of Public Safety
Montpelier, VT 05602   (802) 828-2144

VIRGINIA
Department of State Police
P.O. Box 27472
Richmond, VA 23261   (804) 272-1431

WASHINGTON
State Patrol
General Administration Building
Olympia, WA 98504   (206) 735-6545

WEST VIRGINIA
Department of Public Safety
725 Jefferson Road
South Charleston, WV 25309   (304) 746-2100

WISCONSIN
Enforcement Bureau & State Patrol
4802 Sheboygan Avenue
Madison, WI 53702   (608) 266-3212

WYOMING
Highway Patrol
P.O. Box 1708
Cheyenne, WY 82001   (307) 777-7301

Appendix 6

State
Vital Statistics
Offices

ALABAMA
Bureau of Vital Statistics
State Department of Public Health
Montgomery, AL 36130

ALASKA
Department of Health
Bureau of Vital Statistics
Pouch H 02G
Juneau, AK 99811

AMERICAN SAMOA
Registrar of Vital Statistics
Government of American Samoa
Pago Pago, American Samoa 96799

ARIZONA
Vital Records Section
Arizona Department of Health
P.O. Box 3887
Phoenix, AZ 85030

ARKANSAS
Division of Vital Records
4815 West Markham Street
Little Rock, AR 72201

CALIFORNIA
Vital Statistics Section
410 N Street
Sacramento, CA 95814

CANAL ZONE
Panama Canal Commission
Vital Statistics Clerk
APO Miami, FL 34011

COLORADO
Vital Records Section
4210 East 11th Avenue
Denver, CO 80220

CONNECTICUT
Vital Records Section
150 Washington Street
Hartford, CT 06106

DELAWARE
Bureau of Vital Statistics
Jesse S. Cooper Bldg.
Dover, DE 19901

DISTRICT OF COLUMBIA
Vital Records Branch
425 I Street N.W., Room 309
Washington, DC 20001

FLORIDA
Department of Health
Office of Vital Statistics
P.O. Box 210
Jacksonville, FL 32231

GEORGIA
Vital Records Unit
47 Trinity Avenue S.W.
Atlanta, GA 30334

GUAM
Office of Vital Statistics
P.O. Box 2816
Agana, Guam 96910

HAWAII
Vital Statistics Office
P.O. Box 3378
Honolulu, HI 96801

IDAHO
Bureau of Vital Statistics
Statehouse
Boise, ID 83720

ILLINOIS
Office of Vital Records
535 West Jefferson Street
Springfield, IL 62671

INDIANA
Division of Vital Records
P.O. Box 1964
Indianapolis, IN 46206

IOWA
Vital Records Section
Lucas State Office Building
Des Moines, IA 50319

KANSAS
Office of Vital Statistics
Forbes Field Building 740
Topeka, KS 66620

KENTUCKY
Office of Vital Statistics
275 East Main Street
Frankfort, KY 40621

LOUISIANA
Division of Vital Statistics
P.O. Box 60630
New Orleans, LA 70160

MAINE
Office of Vital Statistics
Human Services Building, Station 2
Augusta, ME 04333

MARYLAND
Division of Vital Statistics
P.O. Box 13146
Baltimore, MD 21203

MASSACHUSETTS
Registry of Vital Records
150 Tremont Street
Boston, MA 02111

MICHIGAN
Office of The State Registrar
3500 North Logan Road
Lansing, MI 48909

MINNESOTA
Section of Vital Statistics
717 Delaware Street S.E.
P.O. Box 9441
Minneapolis, MN 55440

MISSISSIPPI
Vital Records
P.O. Box 1700
Jackson, MS 39215

MISSOURI
Bureau of Vital Records
P.O. Box 570
Jefferson City, MO 65102

MONTANA
Bureau of Statistics
State Department of Health
Helena, MT 59620

NEBRASKA
Bureau of Vital Statistics
P.O. Box 95007
Lincoln, NE 68509

NEVADA
Vital Statistics
Capital Complex
Carson City, NV 89710

NEW HAMPSHIRE
Bureau of Vital Records
Hazen Drive
Concord, NH 03301

NEW JERSEY
Bureau of Vital Statistics
CN 360
Trenton, NJ 08625

NEW MEXICO
Vital Statistics Bureau
P.O. Box 968
Santa Fe, NM 87504

NEW YORK
Bureau of Vital Records
Tower Building
Empire State Plaza
Albany, NY 12237

NEW YORK CITY
Bureau of Vital Records
125 Worth Street
New York, NY 10013

NORTH CAROLINA
Vital Records Branch
P.O. Box 2091
Raleigh, NC 27602

NORTH DAKOTA
Division of Vital Records
Bismarck, ND 58505

OHIO
Division of Vital Statistics
65 South Front Street
Columbus, OH 43215

OKLAHOMA
Vital Records Section
P.O. Box 53551
Oklahoma City, OK 73152

OREGON
Vital Statistics Section
P.O. Box 116
Portland, OR 97207

PENNSYLVANIA
Division of Vital Statistics
P.O. Box 1528
New Castle, PA 16103

PUERTO RICO
Vital Statistics
Department of Health
San Juan, PR 00908

RHODE ISLAND
Division of Vital Statistics
75 Davis Street
Providence, RI 02980

SOUTH CAROLINA
Office of Vital Records
600 Bull Street
Columbia, SC 29201

SOUTH DAKOTA
  Health Statistics
  Joe Foss Office Building
  Pierre, SD 57501

TENNESSEE
  Vital Records
  Cordell Hull Building
  Nashville, TN

TEXAS
  Bureau of Vital Statistics
  1100 West 49th Street
  Austin, TX 78756

UTAH
  Bureau of Health Statistics
  P.O. Box 2500
  Salt Lake City, UT 84110

VERMONT
  Vital Records Section
  Box 70
  60 Main Street
  Burlington, VT 05402

WASHINGTON
  Vital Records
  P.O. Box 9709
  Olympia, WA 98504

WEST VIRGINIA
  Division of Vital Statistics
  State Office Building Three
  Charleston, WV 25305

WISCONSIN
Bureau of Health Statistics
P.O. Box 309
Madison, WI 53701

WYOMING
Vital Records Section
Hathaway Building
Cheyenne, WY 82002

Appendix $\boxed{7}$

State Regulated Businesses

Aircraft Repair
Airports
Alarm Installers
Alcohol Sales
Architects
Auctioneers
Auto Inspectors
Auto Wreckers
Automotive Repair
   Shops
Bankers
Barbers & Beauticians
Bill Collectors
Builders & Carpenters
Building Contractors
Building Wreckers
Carpet Cleaners
CPAs
Child Care & Day Care
Chiropractors
Dentists
Doctors

Electricians
Engineers
   (Professional)
Explosives Technicians
Explosive Storage
Food Processing
Fuel Dispensers
Fuel Storage
Fuel Transportation
Furniture Manu-
   facturing
Gaming & Gambling
Garment Cleaners
Insurance Brokers
Investigators
Laboratories
Lawyers
Marriage Counselors
Mattress Rebuilders
Meat Packers
Meat Storage
Mechanics (Smog)

Mining
Movie Theaters
Notary Publics
Nurses
Nursing Homes
Oil Drilling
Painting Contractors
Pawnbrokers
Personnel Placement
Pet Groomers
Pest Controllers
Pharmacists
Pilots
Plumbers
Police (Private)
Polluters
Process Servers
Public Transportation
Real Estate Broker

Real Estate Salesman
Restaurants
Scrap Dealers
Security Guards
Service Stations
Stock Brokers
Surveyors
Taxis
Teachers
Therapists
Timbering
Trade Schools
Waste Disposal
Waste Removal
Waste Storage
Waste (Hazardous)
Water Taxis
Weights & Measures

Appendix 8

State Tax Records

ALABAMA
Department of Revenue
Administrative Building
Montgomery, AL 36130   (205) 832-5780

ALASKA
Department of Revenue
Pouch S
Juneau, AK 99811   (907) 465-2300

ARIZONA
Department of Revenue
1700 West Washington, Room 202
Phoenix, AZ 85007   (602) 255-3572

ARKANSAS
Revenue Division
7th & High Streets
Little Rock, AR 72203   (501) 371-1535

CALIFORNIA
Franchise Tax Board
Aerojet Center
Sacramento, CA 95857   (916) 355-0292

COLORADO
Department of Revenue
1375 Sherman, Room 46
Denver, CO 80203   (303) 866-3091

CONNECTICUT
Department of Revenue Services
92 Farmington Avenue
Hartford, CT 06106   (203) 566-7120

DELAWARE
Department of Finance
Carvel State Office Building
Wilmington, DE 19801   (302) 571-3316

DISTRICT OF COLUMBIA
Department of Finance and Revenue
300 Indiana Avenue N.W.
Washington, DC 20001   (202) 727-6083

FLORIDA
Department of Revenue
Carlton Building
Tallahassee, FL 32301   (904) 488-5050

GEORGIA
Department of Revenue
270 Washington Street S.W.
Atlanta, GA 30334   (404) 656-4015

HAWAII
Department of Taxation
425 South Queen Street
Honolulu, HI 96813 (808) 548-7650

IDAHO
State Tax Commission
700 West State Street
Boise, ID 83720 (208) 334-4635

ILLINOIS
Department of Revenue
1500 South 9th Street
Springfield, IL 62708 (217) 782-6330

INDIANA
Department of Revenue
Room 202, State Office Building
Indianapolis, IN 46204 (317) 232-2101

IOWA
Department of Revenue
Hoover State Office Building
Des Moines, IA 50319 (515) 281-3204

KANSAS
Department of Revenue
State Office Building, 2nd Floor
Topeka, KS 66612 (913) 296-3809

KENTUCKY
Revenue Cabinet
Capitol Annex
Frankfort, KY 40601 (502) 564-3226

LOUISIANA
Department of Revenue & Taxation
P.O. Box 201
Baton Rouge, LA 70821   (504) 925-7537

MAINE
Bureau of Taxation
State House Station #24
Augusta, ME 04333   (207) 289-2076

MARYLAND
Comptroller of the Treasury
P.O. Box 466
Baltimore, MD 21204   (301) 289-2076

MASSACHUSETTS
Department of Revenue
100 Cambridge Street, Room 806
Boston, MA 02204   (617) 727-4201

MICHIGAN
Bureau of Collections
Treasury Building
Lansing, MI 48909   (517) 373-3401

MINNESOTA
Department of Revenue
Centennial Office Building
St. Paul, MN 55145   (612) 296-3401

MISSISSIPPI
State Tax Commission
102 Woolfolk Building
Jackson, MS 39201   (601) 359-1098

MISSOURI
Department of Revenue
P.O. Box 311
Jefferson City, MO 65105   (314) 751-4450

MONTANA
Department of Revenue
Capitol Station
Helena, MT 59620   (406) 444-2460

NEBRASKA
Department of Revenue
P.O. Box 94818
Lincoln, NE 68509-4818   (402) 471-2971

NEVADA
Department of Taxation
1340 South Curry Street
Carson City, NV 89710   (702) 885-4892

NEW HAMPSHIRE
Department of Revenue Administration
P.O. Box 467
Concord, NH 03301   (603) 271-2191

NEW JERSEY
Division of Taxation
CN 246
Trenton, NJ 08645   (609) 292-5185

NEW MEXICO
Taxation & Revenue Department
P.O. Box 630
Santa Fe, NM 87509   (505) 988-2290

NEW YORK
Department of Taxation & Finance
Campus, Tax & Finance Building
Albany, NY 12227   (518) 438-8581

NORTH CAROLINA
Department of Revenue
2 South Salisbury Street
Raleigh, NC 27611   (919) 733-7211

NORTH DAKOTA
Tax Department
State Capitol, 8th Floor
Bismarck, ND 58505   (701) 224-2770

OHIO
Department of Taxation
30 East Broad Street, 22nd Floor
Columbus, OH 43215   (614) 466-2166

OKLAHOMA
Tax Commission
Conners Building, Room 343
Oklahoma City, OK 73105   (405) 521-3115

OREGON
Department of Revenue
955 Center Street N.E.
Salem, OR 97310   (503) 378-3363

PENNSYLVANIA
Department of Revenue
Strawberry Square, 11th Floor
Harrisburg, PA 17120   (717) 783-3680

RHODE ISLAND
Division of Taxation
289 Promenade Street
North Scituate, RI 02903   (401) 277-3050

SOUTH CAROLINA
Tax Commission
P.O. Box 125
Columbia, SC 29214   (803) 758-2691

SOUTH DAKOTA
Department of Revenue
Kneip Building, 3rd Floor
Pierre, SD 57501   (605) 773-3311

TENNESSEE
Department of Revenue
927 Andrew Jackson
   State Office Building
Nashville, TN 37219   (615) 741-2461

TEXAS
Public Accounts
LBJ Building, Room 104
Austin, TX 78774   (512) 475-1900

UTAH
Tax Commission
160 East 300 South
Salt Lake City, UT 84134-4000   (801) 530-6088

VERMONT
Department of Taxes
Pavilion Office Building
Montpelier, VT 05602   (802) 828-2505

VIRGINIA
Department of Taxation
2220 West Broad Street
Richmond, VA 23220 (804) 257-8005

WASHINGTON
Department of Revenue
General Administration Building AX-02
Olympia, WA 98504 (206) 753-5574

WEST VIRGINIA
Tax Department
1800 East Washington Street, Building 1
Charleston, WV 25305 (304) 348-2501

WISCONSIN
Department of Revenue
P.O. Box 8933
Madison, WI 53708 (608) 266-6466

WYOMING
State Tax Commission
2200 Carey Avenue
Cheyenne, WY 82002 (307) 777-7961

Appendix $\boxed{9}$

Military Record Request Form

See pages 112 and 113.

112 BE YOUR OWN DICK

REQUEST PERTAINING TO MILITARY RECORDS | *Please read instructions on the reverse. If more space is needed, use plain paper.*

PRIVACY ACT OF 1974 COMPLIANCE INFORMATION. The following information is provided in accordance with 5 U.S.C. 552a(e)(3) and applies to this form. Authority for collection of the information is 44 U.S.C. 2907, 3101, and 3103, and E.O. 9397 of November 22, 1943. Disclosure of the information is voluntary. The principal purpose of the information is to assist the facility servicing the records in locating and verifying the correctness of the requested records or information to answer your inquiry. Routine uses of the information as established and published in accordance with 5 U.S.C.a(e)(4)(D)

include the transfer of relevant information to appropriate Federal, State, local, or foreign agencies for use in civil, criminal, or regulatory investigations or prosecution. In addition, this form will be filed with the appropriate military records and may be transferred along with the record to another agency in accordance with the routine uses established by the agency which maintains the record. If the requested information is not provided, it may not be possible to service your inquiry.

SECTION I—INFORMATION NEEDED TO LOCATE RECORDS (Furnish as much as possible)

1. NAME USED DURING SERVICE *(Last, first, and middle)*	2. SOCIAL SECURITY NO.	3. DATE OF BIRTH	4. PLACE OF BIRTH

5. ACTIVE SERVICE, PAST AND PRESENT   (For an effective records search, it is important that ALL service be shown below)

BRANCH OF SERVICE *(Also, show last organization, if known)*	DATES OF ACTIVE SERVICE		Check one		SERVICE NUMBER DURING THIS PERIOD
	DATE ENTERED	DATE RELEASED	OFFICER	ENLISTED	

6. RESERVE SERVICE, PAST OR PRESENT   If "none," check here ▶ ☐

a. BRANCH OF SERVICE	b. DATES OF MEMBERSHIP		c. Check one		d. SERVICE NUMBER DURING THIS PERIOD
	FROM	TO	OFFICER ☐	ENLISTED ☐	

7. NATIONAL GUARD MEMBERSHIP   (Check one):   a. ARMY ☐   b. AIR FORCE ☐   c. NONE ☐

d. STATE	e. ORGANIZATION	f. DATES OF MEMBERSHIP		g. Check one		h. SERVICE NUMBER DURING THIS PERIOD
		FROM	TO	OFFICER ☐	ENLISTED ☐	

8. IS SERVICE PERSON DECEASED ☐ YES ☐ NO If "yes," enter date of death.	9. IS (WAS) INDIVIDUAL A MILITARY RETIREE OR FLEET RESERVIST ☐ YES ☐ NO

SECTION II—REQUEST

1. EXPLAIN WHAT INFORMATION OR DOCUMENTS YOU NEED; OR, CHECK ITEM 2; OR, COMPLETE ITEM 3	2. IF YOU ONLY NEED A STATEMENT OF SERVICE · check here ☐

3. LOST SEPARATION DOCUMENT REPLACEMENT REQUEST *(Complete a or b, and c.)*

☐ a. REPORT OF SEPARATION (DD Form 214 or equivalent)	YEAR ISSUED	This contains information normally needed to determine eligibility for benefits. It may be furnished only to the veteran, the surviving next of kin, or to a representative with veteran's signed release (item 5 of this form).
☐ b. DISCHARGE CERTIFICATE	YEAR ISSUED	This shows only the date and character at discharge. It is of little value in determining eligibility for benefits. It may be issued only to veterans discharged honorably or under honorable conditions; or, if deceased, to the surviving spouse.

c. EXPLAIN HOW SEPARATION DOCUMENT WAS LOST

4. EXPLAIN PURPOSE FOR WHICH INFORMATION OR DOCUMENTS ARE NEEDED	6. REQUESTER
	a. IDENTIFICATION (check appropriate box)
	☐ Same person identified in Section I ☐ Surviving spouse
	☐ Next of kin (relationship) _____
	☐ Other (specify) _____
	b. SIGNATURE (see instruction 3 on reverse side) DATE OF REQUEST

5. RELEASE AUTHORIZATION, IF REQUIRED (Read instruction 3 on reverse side)	7. Please type or print clearly — COMPLETE RETURN ADDRESS
I hereby authorize release of the requested information/documents to the person indicated at right (item 7).	Name, number and street, city, State and ZIP code
VETERAN SIGN HERE ▶	
(If signed by other than veteran show relationship to veteran.)	TELEPHONE NO. (include area code) ▶

INSTRUCTIONS

1. Information needed to locate records. Certain identifying information is necessary to determine the location of an individual's record of military service. Please give careful consideration to and answer each item on this form. If you do not have and cannot obtain the information for an item, show "NA," meaning the information is "not available." Include as much of the requested information as you can. This will help us to give you the best possible service.

2. Charges for service. A nominal fee is charged for certain types of service. In most instances service fees cannot be determined in advance. If your request involves a service fee you will be notified as soon as that determination is made.

3. Restrictions on release of information. Information from records of military personnel is released subject to restrictions imposed by the military departments consistent with the provisions of the Freedom of Information Act of 1967 (as amended in 1974) and the Privacy Act of 1974. A service person has access to almost any information contained in his own record. The next of kin, if the veteran is deceased, and Federal officers for official purposes, are authorized to receive information from a military service or medical record only as specified in the above cited Acts. Other requesters must have the release authorization, in item 5 of the form, signed by the veteran or, if deceased, by the next of kin. Employers

and others needing proof of military service are expected to accept the information shown on documents issued by the Armed Forces at the time a service person is separated.

4. Location of military personnel records. The various categories of military personnel records are described in the chart below. For each category there is a code number which indicates the address at the bottom of the page to which this request should be sent. For each military service there is a note explaining approximately how long the records are held by the military service before they are transferred to the National Personnel Records Center, St. Louis. Please read these notes carefully and make sure you send your inquiry to the right address. Please note especially that the record is not sent to the National Personnel Records Center as 'ong as the person retains any sort of reserve obligation, whether drilling or non-drilling.

(If the person has two or more periods of service within the same branch, send your request to the office having the record for the last period of service.)

5. Definitions for abbreviations used below:
NPRC — National Personnel Records Center   PERS — Personnel Records
TDRL — Temporary Disability Retirement List   MED — Medical Records

SERVICE	NOTE: (See paragraph 4 above.)	CATEGORY OF RECORDS	WHERE TO WRITE ADDRESS CODE ▼
AIR FORCE (USAF)	Except for TDRL and general officers retired with pay, Air Force records are transferred to NPRC from Code 1, 90 days after separation and from Code 2, 150 days after separation.	Active members (includes National Guard on active duty in the Air Force, TDRL, and general officers retired with pay	1
		Reserve, retired reservist in nonpay status, current National Guard officers not on active duty in Air Force, and National Guard released from active duty in Air Force	2
		Current National Guard enlisted not on active duty in Air Force	13
		Discharged, deceased, and retired with pay	14
COAST GUARD (USCG)	Coast Guard officer and enlisted records are transferred to NPRC 7 months after separation.	Active, reserve, and TDRL members	3
		Discharged, deceased, and retired members *(see next item)*	14
		Officers separated before 1/1/29 and enlisted personnel separated before 1/1/15	6
MARINE CORPS (USMC)	Marine Corps records are transferred to NPRC between 6 and 9 months after separation.	Active, TDRL, and Selected Marine Corps Reserve members	4
		Individual Ready Reserve and Fleet Marine Corps Reserve members	5
		Discharged, deceased, and retired members *(see next item)*	14
		Members separated before 1/1/1905	6
ARMY (USA)	Army records are transferred to NPRC as follows: Active Army and Individual Ready Reserve Control Groups: About 60 days after separation. U.S. Army Reserve Troop Unit personnel: About 120 to 180 days after separation.	Reserve, living retired members, retired general officers, and active duty records of current National Guard members who performed service in the U.S. Army before 7/1/72.*	7
		Active officers (including National Guard on active duty in the U.S. Army)	8
		Active enlisted (including National Guard on active duty in the U.S. Army) and enlisted TDRL	9
		Current National Guard officers not on active duty in the U.S. Army	12
		Current National Guard enlisted not on active duty in the U.S. Army	13
		Discharged and deceased members *(see next item)*	14
		Officers separated before 7/1/17 and enlisted separated before 11/1/12	6
		Officers and warrant officers TDRL	8
NAVY (USN)	Navy records are transferred to NPRC 6 months after retirement or complete separation.	Active members (including reservists on duty) — PERS and MED	10
		Discharged, deceased, retired (with and without pay) less than six months. TDRL, drilling and nondrilling reservists	PERS ONLY — 10 / MED ONLY — 11
		Discharged, deceased, retired (with and without pay) more than six months *(see next item)* — PERS & MED	14
		Officers separated before 1/1/03 and enlisted separated before 1/1/1886 — PERS and MED	6

*Code 12 applies to active duty records of current National Guard officers who performed service in the U.S. Army after 6/30/72
Code 13 applies to active duty records of current National Guard enlisted members who performed service in the U.S. Army after 6/30/72

ADDRESS LIST OF CUSTODIANS (BY CODE NUMBERS SHOWN ABOVE) — Where to write / send this form for each category of records

1	Air Force Manpower and Personnel Center Military Personnel Records Division Randolph AFB, TX 78150-6001	**5**	Marine Corps Reserve Support Center 10950 El Monte Overland Park, KS 66211-1408	**8**	USA MILPERCEN ATTN: DAPC-MSR 200 Stoval Street Alexandria, VA 22332-0400	**12**	Army National Guard Personnel Center Columbia Pike Office Building 5600 Columbia Pike Falls Church, VA 22041
2	Air Reserve Personnel Center Denver, CO 80280-5000	**6**	Military Archives Division National Archives and Records Administration Washington, DC 20408	**9**	Commander U.S. Army Enlisted Records and Evaluation Center Ft Benjamin Harrison, IN 46249-5301	**13**	The Adjutant General (of the appropriate State, DC, or Puerto Rico)
3	Commandant U.S. Coast Guard Washington, DC 20593-0001	**7**	Commander U.S. Army Reserve Personnel Center ATTN: DARP-PAS 9700 Page Boulevard St. Louis, MO 63132-5200	**10**	Commander Naval Military Personnel Command ATTN: NMPC-036 Washington, DC 20370-5036	**14**	National Personnel Records Center (Military Personnel Records) 9700 Page Boulevard St. Louis, MO 63132
4	Commandant of the Marine Corps (Code MMRB-10) Headquarters, U.S. Marine Corps Washington, DC 20380-0001			**11**	Naval Reserve Personnel Center New Orleans, LA 70146-5000		

490-498 (m)

STANDARD FORM 180 BACK (Rev. 7-84)

YOU WILL ALSO WANT TO READ:

☐ **55083 ESPIONAGE: DOWN & DIRTY**, *by Tony Lesce.* What's spying really like? Read this book and find out. Covers recruiting, training, infiltration, payment (including sex), evacuation, what happens when a spy is exposed, and more. Also reveals the exploits of many notorious spies: The Walker Spy Ring, "Falcon and Snowman," The Pollard Case, and many others. *1991, 5½ x 8½, 180 pp, soft cover. $17.95.*

☐ **61061 HOW TO FIND MISSING PERSONS**, *by Ronald George Eriksen 2.* The classic book on hunting down anyone, anywhere. The author is a missing persons investigator who shares his hard-earned tips for finding people who do not want to be found. Shows how to use public and private records to track someone. Includes many practical ruses to get information from those who are unwilling to divulge it. An essential book for any investigator, and for those who want to preserve their privacy. *1984, 5½ x 8½, 102 pp, illustrated, soft cover. $9.95*

☐ **55072 THE MUCKRAKER'S MANUAL, How to Do Your Own Investigative Reporting**, *by M. Harry.* How to dig out the dirt on anyone! Written for investigative reporters exposing political corruption, the detailed professional investigative techniques are useful to any investigation. Developing "inside" sources ● Getting documents ● Incredible ruses that really work ● Interviewing techniques ● Infiltration ● When to stop an investigation ● Protecting your sources ● And much more. *1984, 5½ x 8½, 148 pp, illustrated, soft cover. $12.95*

☐ **55052 SHADOWING AND SURVEILLANCE**, *by Burt Rapp.* This is a no-nonsense guide to shadowing and surveillance techniques with an emphasis on do-it-yourself, low-support methods. Tailing on foot and in a car ● How to lose a tail ● Using decoys and disguises ● Searching property ● Photographic surveillance techniques ● How to conduct a stakeout ● And much more. *1986, 5½ x 8½, 136 pp, illustrated, soft cover. $14.95*

And much more! We offer the very finest in controversial and unusual books — please turn to our catalog announcement on the next page.

_____BYOD2

LOOMPANICS UNLIMITED
PO Box 1197/Port Townsend, WA 98368

Please send me the titles I have checked above. I have enclosed $_____ (including $4.00 for shipping and handling of 1 to 3 titles, $6.00 for 4 or more).

Name _____

Address _____

City/State/Zip _____

(Washington residents include 7.8% sales tax.)